Faith and Justice

Top photo:
Part of the audience
at the 1981
Loyola-Baumgarth Symposium

Bottom photo:
Father Raymond Baumhart, S.J.,
Loyola's President, and
Dr. James Wiser

The 1981
Loyola-Baumgarth Symposium
on Values and Ethics

Faith and Justice

March 24 and 31 and April 8, 1981

Walter P. Krolikowski, S.J., editor
Professor of Foundations of Education
Loyola University of Chicago

Loyola University Press

Chicago, 1982

ISBN 0-8294-0397-3

Contents

Introduction

Walter P. Krolikowski, S.J.

Educational institutions are committed to an exalted view of the position of language in the lives of mankind. Educators see rational speech as both illuminator and healer: illuminator shedding light on the obscurities and confusions of our daily lives, healer of the divisions and wounds suffered by mankind frequently enough and paradoxically enough because the power of speech has been used badly. If people would only talk to each other—and listen to each other!

Educational institutions, however, are wise enough to know that shared reflection and thought, indispensable though they are, guarantee the success of no human enterprise. Only reflection that directs the actions of persons deeply committed to sharing their destinies with one another ultimately makes a difference.

There are instances of reflection flowing into loving action in every university. At Loyola, for example, medical science is at the service of the ill. Law students operate a neighborhood law clinic. Students of social work and education work in human services and welfare agencies and in schools. Skilled help is available for deeply disturbed children. Money is raised for the poor of the Third World.

But more often the members of the university community must be content to speak with each other in hope. In classrooms and on certain set occasions they reflect and share their reflection with each other on the pressing problems of the present era. They do not see this kind of sharing as an empty exercise.

Speech does have a power of its own, a dynamism that frequently leads to actions at later times and in other places that the speakers themselves could not have foreseen. That result is the hoped-for, prayed-for consequence one can never demand as one's just reward for rational speech.

It is in this spirit of hope that the university community at Loyola gathered for the 1980 Loyola-Baumgarth Symposium on Values and Ethics, *Ethics on a Catholic University Campus.* In that same spirit, they gathered again this past academic year for the 1981 Loyola-Baumgarth Symposium on Values and Ethics, *Faith and Justice,* the papers of which form the body of this volume.

Given the nature of Loyola as a Catholic and Jesuit university, the theme of this year's symposium was easily arrived at. In 1975 the Jesuits had formulated yet again the basic choice that specifies their identity as Jesuits: "The service of faith and the promotion of justice cannot be for us simply one ministry among others. It must be the integrating factor of all our ministries; and not only of our ministries but of our inner life as individuals, as communities, and as a worldwide brotherhood." It was an easy inference that a similar concern for faith and justice ought to be a signalizing mark of a Jesuit university. This inference was all the easier to make because concerned persons around the world—a world with little or "no knowledge of God"; a world forgetful of the "mystery of man's ultimate meaning," dignity, and beauty; a world "increasingly interdependent but tragically divided by injustice"—have also come to see the crucial importance of faith and justice. And these people look to the university as a resource and support in their efforts to make operative faith and justice throughout the world.

As a result Loyola University's Committee on Values and Ethics, under the leadership of Dr. James D. Barry, invited members of Loyola University's community to ask what Loyola's role ought to be in bringing faith and justice to the various communities it serves: the university community itself; its neighborhood, city, and country; Third World nations and the world at large. Members of the Loyola community were asked to present answers to the question: How do we educate for faith and justice in the face of declining world resources, in the face of increasing unemployment, in the face of increasing population, in the face of professional pressures, in the face of technological societies?

The response, in the form of abstracts of possible papers and presentations, was large and prompt. The Committee on Values and Ethics was able to prepare an elaborate and thoughtful program.

A word on the program may be helpful. The reach of the papers is enormous. A large university inevitably has the resources for a far-reaching discussion. Theology, sociology, anthropology, political science, psychiatry, communication arts, nursing, biology, education, and university ministry—each had its contribution to make. Some readers will undoubtedly be drawn to the papers of Dr. Robert Ludwig, Dr. Thomas Cunningham, and Father Gerald Grosh for their theological insights. Others will find of great moment the sociological analysis by Dr. Kirsten Grønbjerg, Dr. Kathleen McCourt, and Dr. Robert McNamara of the problems of upward mobility for black Americans, or the analyses of Father Joseph Small and Dr. Ralph Rossum on the need for ethical standards in public officials. Still others will be attracted to the papers of Dr. Paul Breidenbach and Father Joseph Boel on the problems of the Third World. The discussions, ranging from the problems of internal housekeeping within the university to those of worldwide concern, are fine examples of the quality of university discussions. They ask the right questions; they suggest possible approaches for thinking those questions through; they leave the reader enlightened and, if anything, more uncomfortable than before.

What remains to be said is most pleasant. The 1981 Loyola-Baumgarth Symposium on Values and Ethics, as that of the previous year, was underwritten by a grant from the John Baumgarth Foundation. Loyola University is most grateful for this assistance. The members of the Planning Committee for the Symposium were: Dr. James Barry; Ms. Marilyn Birchfield; Dr. William Donnelly; Dr. Alan Fredian; Ms. Maureen Fuechtmann; Rev. Walter Krolikowski, S.J.; Mr. Joseph Lassner; Rev. Thomas McMahon, C.S.V.; Mr. Charles Murdock; Rev. Joseph Small, S.J.; Ms. Jan Slattery; and Dr. Patricia Werhane.

The Committee will be most happy if the Symposium has in some small measure been a response to the call of Pope Paul VI in his encyclical *Populorum Progressio*.

We must make haste. Too many are suffering. There are certainly situations whose injustice cries to heaven. A renewed consciousness of the demands of the Gospel make it a duty for the church to put herself at the service of all, to convince all that solidarity in action is a matter of urgency.

Ultimately, the university must do more than think through the problems of faith and justice, enormous as that task is; it must itself be a model of faith and justice, and it must promote faith and justice, directly through its own mission or indirectly through the subsequent activities of its students, wherever it can reach and have an influence. "Paul did the planting, Apollos did the watering, but God makes things grow."

Words of Welcome

Father Raymond C. Baumhart, S.J.

When I opened the 1980 Loyola-Baumgarth Symposium twelve months ago, I felt good about the situation. Today, March 24, 1981, I feel better. Let me explain why.

A year ago we had already had much activity in what I will call Loyola's renewed emphasis on values and ethics. Over one hundred university groups (various administrative units and standing committees) had discussed the university-wide Planning Committee statement on the importance of values and ethics at Loyola and had drawn up thoughtful reports. And we were giving a certain focus to events by the 1980 symposium on *Ethics on a Catholic University Campus*. And so I felt good on that occasion as I opened that symposium and asked people to make suggestions about how we at this Jesuit and Catholic university might better institutionalize, further develop, this renewed thrust on values and ethics.

What has happened since last March? We have established a new university standing committee, the Committee on Values and Ethics. We have published proceedings of the 1980 Loyola-Baumgarth Symposium: *Ethics on a Catholic University Campus*. We have successfully launched a series of informal discussions on texts that deal with values and ethics; the first text, which was discussed recently during four sessions, was Sissela Bok's *Lying*. We have under way at our Medical Center the 1981 Medical Humanities Clinical Colloquies—this time on "Power in Medicine." We have done other things; we have other plans.

And of course today we open the 1981 Loyola-Baumgarth Symposium on Values and Ethics—this year on the theme "Faith and Justice," a theme that will allow us to confront a profoundly important and complex topic, one in keeping with Loyola's best traditions.

The choice of this theme stemmed from an international meeting, the 32nd General Congregation of the Society of Jesus. That meeting—it lasted more than three months—produced a series of documents on the challenges of our times and the Jesuit response. One phrase has come to epitomize the message of that General Congregation: "the service of faith and the promotion of justice." What we will be hearing at these several sessions is thoughtful reflection by some of the ablest members of the Loyola community on a variety of facets of this jewel of a theme, "Faith and Justice."

Yes, I felt good a year ago. I feel better today—for the reasons I have noted and for another important reason: your presence. It is good to see you here. Welcome to the 1981 Loyola-Baumgarth Symposium.

Faith and Justice

FIRST GENERAL SESSION
Dr. Robert Ludwig
Dr. James Wiser
Father Francis L. Filas, S.J.
(from left to right)

The Politics of Compassion: Grace and Reconciliation in Society

Dr. Robert Ludwig
University Ministry

Moderator
Dr. James L. Wiser
Chairman, Department of Political Science

Responder
Father Francis L. Filas, S.J.
Department of Theology

Dr. Wiser: Thank you, Father Baumhart.

The general theme of this symposium is "Faith and Justice." The particular theme of this session is "The Politics of Compassion: Grace and Reconciliation in Society." Presenting this session's paper is Dr. Robert Ludwig of the University Ministry. He is also an adjunct professor with the Institute of Pastoral Studies. Dr. Ludwig earned his Ph.D. degree in theology from the Aquinas Institute of Theology; his dissertation was on the thought of Daniel Berrigan. Prior to coming to Loyola in 1979, Dr. Ludwig taught religious studies at Clark College, St. Thomas Seminary, the University of Denver, and the University of Colorado at Boulder.

Responding to the presentation will be Father Francis Filas. Father Filas has been with Loyola's Theology Department since 1950. During eight of these thirty years

1

he served as department chairman. His scholarly interests range from biblical geography and moral theology to research on the authenticity of the Shroud of Turin.

I now present Dr. Robert Ludwig.

Dr. Ludwig: I am delighted to have this opportunity to present publicly my thoughts on a topic which has absorbed a good deal of my time and energy for the past eighteen years, ever since I first heard John Howard Griffin discuss religion and racism at Conception Seminary in Conception, Missouri in 1963.

Before I move into my presentation as such, I would like to give you a quick outline of what I intend to say. I will begin with some introductory comments on resurrection faith including a story from Father Daniel Berrigan. Then I will proceed with a brief discussion on the new theology of hope, as a basis for the new correlation of theology and politics which is taking place in our time. After a brief summary of the critique which this theology presents for a so-called traditional theology, I would like to move into a brief exposé of current political theology as an attempt to criticize present social structures and imagine new social paradigms. Finally, I will conclude with a summary of the social teachings of the popes during this century.

In my paper I refer a number of times to the word *eschatological.* It might be useful to explain quickly that it is a term we use to refer to the ultimate future, to the end, to the goal of history.

The Politics of Compassion: Grace and Reconciliation in Society
Dr. Robert Ludwig

A recent issue of *Sojourners* magazine contains an excerpt from Daniel Berrigan's newest book, *Ten Commandments for the Long Haul.* Berrigan raises the question, "What Do We Expect of Christ?" and as a way of testing a response to that question, he conjures up an image of "the unlikeliest event conceivable in this world." In this image the "death of a dear one has occurred; shocking, unexpected. Shortly thereafter, friends stand grieving at an open grave. . . . Suddenly this scene of mute grief is brought to a halt, invaded, confronted. Someone is in the midst of the mourners, someone who is not mourning. The tears, the vertigo, the emotional welter of death, halt in midair. Someone stands there. He is also a friend, but he is no mourner. Instead, he commands attention, shockingly, with power. 'Lazarus, come forth.' We are fascinated, horrified even, attention wildly divided. The mouth of the grave, the face of the living? Then the unthinkable occurs. A dead man stands in our midst, living." We probably hear this story today with incredulity. We dismiss it quickly, think it absurd. Berrigan himself sympathizes: "We commonly judge that we will have to deal only with death; and that, we say, is quite enough. Never in this world will we witness death undone, the once dead standing in our midst, and we grown wild, beside ourselves with joy. Never. And yet," he continues, ". . . it is against such an event as this that our expectation of Christ . . . must be measured. The unlikeliest event in the world. The event we will never see with our mortal eyes. The event we only hear of; one that we must take on the word of others, and they removed from us by nearly infinite vistas, centuries."[1]

Berrigan's query, "What do we expect of Christ?" and his story-response are designed as his attempt to explain why he, his brother Philip, and six others entered the General Electric re-entry systems assembly site in King of Prussia, Pennsylvania, in September 1980, damaging two Mark 12A re-entry vehicle cones and pouring blood on technical blueprints. I cite the *Sojourners* essay, not to defend that action (we can all evaluate that for ourselves), but because I think it serves as a splendid point of departure for these discussions on "Faith and Justice." It is such because it raises the issue of faith directly, at the level of personal meaning and hope for the future: do we take Easter seriously? The most unlikely event is, in fact, the center of the Christian story, the very eye through which the Christian is called to see the whole of reality and interpret all of life by. For our purposes, it is also the key to any genuine optimism, before the social and political situation we face today. Do we take Easter seriously? What do we expect of Christ? This issue every generation of Christians has had to struggle with, and no less has our own. Let me suggest that we cannot take it seriously today by relegating it to the distant past (a curious historical event to be dusted and debated from time to time) or by consigning its meaning to an individualistic future (a narcotic pill to be swallowed during difficult times in this life by individuals who seek a happily-ever-after life in a world beyond). Easter is comprehended today in faith and hope at the levels of existential meaning and eschatological expectation.[2] It is a supreme metaphor which opens up the mystery of human existence and destiny, a proclamation about humankind, about the world, about the future. All that separates and injures and destroys has been overcome by what unifies and heals and creates. Faith and hope go together: to believe in the resurrection is to experience reversal and new possibilities; to trust in the God who raised Jesus from the dead is to put our hope in the promises of transformation and new life, to expect a world of freedom and justice and peace, which promises quicken our imaginations. To take Easter seriously—that is, at the level of existential meaning and eschatological hope—implies as well a critique of every boxed-in, closed paradigm of reality, freeing the imagination to transcend the limited worlds of Augustine's Christianity, of Skinner's behaviorism, of Wilson's sociobiology, of every theory of the human person or social existence that denies our capacity for transcendence and new possibilities. Easter, that is, implies an open-ended journey for creation and history, leading us from horizon to horizon, surprising us, shattering ideologies, laying bare the sacred mystery long enough to entice us forward and beyond.

Without such a metaphor we are trapped and cannot go forward. Without Easter we are doomed to cyclical repetition, and we have no reason to hope for an end to injustice, repression, mass violence. Today, without such a metaphor, we face a cosmic grave.

There are many ways that one might choose to present a theological rationale for justice. One could, for example, begin with the Scholastic discussion of natural law theory and make a case for labeling this or that specific relationship or sets of relationships in current society as unjust because contrary to human rights as discerned from the natural law. Or one could attend to specific issues of social injustice by recourse to biblical texts in which precise instances of injustice are so labeled. One could attempt to extend the work of American scholars like John Courtney Murray who bring together the tradition of democratic values and the rights of individuals as these have developed in the American experience with our tradition of Catholic moral theology.[3] Valuable as these approaches may be, they seem inadequate to our purposes in this symposium, at least from my perspective. I prefer to locate our discussion of justice rather in the theological shift that has occurred in Catholic theology and in the Church during this twentieth century. Contemporary theology is caught up in an exciting new direction, that of "incarnational eschatology" (so called because it highlights the divine presence in *this* world, the world of our present experience, and looks forward to the transformation and fulfillment of *this* world in the eschatological future). The passion with which Catholics and other Christians around the globe are today seeking for justice is grounded, not in Scholastic natural law theory, not even in specific biblical texts referring to justice, nor finally in an extension of American democratic ideals. Today's quest for justice is grounded in the experience of grace and reconciliation and a uniquely contemporary human consciousness, and it is grounded in the radical experience of hope for a new world order. I would like to describe this incarnational eschatology and point to the implications of this dramatic theological shift that is taking place in our present century. These implications for sociopolitical life have been decisively developed by the Magisterium in more than twenty years of what is, by almost anyone's standards, a revolution in the Church's social teaching. I would like to extend these implications and make them specific to Loyola, suggesting some possible directions for our life together in Catholic higher education.

Behind the evident changes that mark the Catholic world in our time stands a major theological transition. A new theology of grace has appeared in the twentieth century, challenging the view of God-person-world established at the Council of Trent, and serving as the rationale for the Second Vatican Council and the reformed and renewed Church that continues to develop.[4] This new theology of grace is the basis for a new "political theology" and the new Catholic emphasis on peace and justice in our time. It shifts our imaging of transcendence from a supernatural order beyond space and time to its locations within our historical experience, as the horizon of our individual and collective longing and expectation. It is a switch from the metaphysical dualism of nature and grace to the existential experience of the human spirit and nature itself as constantly engaged in a process of transcendence.

Among the many important Jesuit thinkers who have contributed to the development of this new theology of grace are Henri De Lubac, Teilhard de Chardin, and most notably Karl Rahner. De Lubac published his *Surnaturel: Études Historiques* in 1946 and *Le mystère du Surnaturel* in 1965. He argues that by virtue of creation, on the basis of his being, the human person is effectively called to community with God, the transcendent fulfillment of his longing and happiness. There are two important points in the mainstream of the Christian tradition that have been eclipsed in theological polemics since the Middle Ages. First, grace is a favor given, gratis. Second, it is also the object of a desire rooted deeply in the personal nature of human beings. What humanity yearns for is free gift, and it is because it is free and gratuitous that this gift sates human desire.[5]

Karl Rahner, operating on the level of a basic religious ontology, expanded De Lubac's insights by developing his notion of "the supernatural existential."[6] Rahner argues that an ontological openness to the Absolute exists at the level of human consciousness. Grace is God communicating himself in love to human persons, who have by their very nature the capacity to receive him. God creates a creature whom he can love, and thus the person is created from the start as capacity for God. This is our most human dimension: that we are open to God's free self-communication. Pure nature (nature before grace, or ungraced nature) is only an abstraction and finds no phenomenon in human history that exemplifies it. Rather a real human experience is geared for transcendence: the itch for God's self-communication is "built-in" to who we are as persons. We discover this transcending spirit in our freedom, in our knowing, in our creativity, in love, in resistance to death, and in hoping against all odds. The human self is always moving from horizon to horizon in its journey toward full communion with the self-communicating God. This experience is universal, not limited by the language or conceptual patterns of Christian faith.

Teilhard's writings move the transcendent dimension from its location in the human spirit to a broader context, that of matter itself. For Teilhard all of matter, the whole cosmos, is the field of grace, because all matter has a "within" consciousness. In Teilhard's sweeping vision, which ties Christian eschatology to the process of creative evolution, the gradual unfolding of the universe is a divine process; the world of matter *is* the world of spirit, the space-time continuum in which creation continues is a divine milieu. God, that is, is not above the world, out of this world, beyond this world; rather, God is present *in* the universe from its inception, is the energy that drives evolution forward, and is the center of attraction that pulls us toward our final, unified goal. Again, as in Rahner's view of the human spirit as "supernatural existential," grace is everywhere, wherever evolution pushes onward and upward, toward ultimate unification. The divine presence is not limited by the language of Christian faith or by the acceptance of doctrine, baptismal participation in an institutional church, or even organized religion. It is universal in matter's quest for final unity and thus integral to the whole of creation.[7]

Prolific theologians like Hans Küng and Edward Schillebeeckx, both of whom have written encyclopedic fundamental theologies in recent years, present variations on this same theme. Küng picks up the Pauline and Protestant emphasis on justification by grace through faith, emphasizing the giftness of grace. He calls for a radical trust in God, which is simultaneously a radical trust in humanity, in history, in our ultimate, collective destiny. To trust in the God who raised the Crucified is a call to become radically human. God's will and man's well-being are the same. "Being Christian is not in addition to being human: there is not a Christian level above or below the human. . . . The Christian element is . . . neither a superstructure nor a substructure of the human. It is an elevation or—better—a transfiguration of the human" by virtue of this trust in God.[8]

Undoubtedly the most comprehensive and dramatic attempt to elaborate this new theology of grace by reference to the New Testament texts is the Christological trilogy of Edward Schillebeeckx. According to Schillebeeckx, grace in the New Testament is an experience—what he calls "the soteriological experience," the experience of being saved. This saving experience is reconciliation, forgiveness, and peace; it is liberation from servitude and slavery, liberation *for* community, *for* brotherly love, *for* freedom, *for* the renewal of humankind and the world, *for* life in

7

fullness; it is hope, the experience of promise of eschatological salvation.[9] Grace is experienced as "not only liberation from unjust conditions . . . [but] what men are freed for is itself in turn a command to free men from unjust circumstances."[10] Thus, liberating and reconciling grace frees us for a task which is to be realized in the dimension of future history.

The result of the theological development in the twentieth century is a new "political theology,"[11] an attempt to spell out the practical implications of grace and reconciliation in a corrective way critical of the tendency since the Enlightenment to confine Christian faith to the realm of the private and the personal. The task of deprivatizing Christian faith means extricating *grace* from individualistic categories, announcing again that reconciliation is about humankind, about history, about the future of this world, and announcing this in specific and concrete formulations of reconciliation and hope in the conditions of present-day society. Grace means a new social theory, a new way of structuring human interaction, relationship, responsibility. Johannes Metz, perhaps the chief architect of this new political theology, points out that "the eschatological promises of the biblical tradition—freedom, peace, justice, reconciliation—do not permit themselves to be privatized," but consistently compel us to social responsibility.[12] The role of the Church in this political theology then is not to serve its own self-affirmation, but rather the historical affirmation of the salvation of all persons. The hope the Church announces is not a hope for itself, but for the kingdom of God, and that hope takes the form of a critical liberating function within today's society. Through this function, Christian love is expanded from the interpersonal sphere of the I-Thou to make it effective in its societal dimension as "the unconditional determination to bring justice, liberty, and peace *to the others.*" The sociocritical dynamism of Christian love means a determined criticism of pure power and the structures that maintain injustice and deny fundamental human rights, in an effort to actualize freedom and justice for others. It also means a determined criticism of the categories of "friend-enemy" and systems of violence, in an effort to actualize reconciliation and peace for others.[13]

Political theology, then, leads to the translation of grace and reconciliation into the concrete realities of social existence today through structural criticism and the creation of new paradigms; it leads to the politics of compassion. In his book, *A Spirituality Named Compassion,* Matthew Fox points to the insight of solidarity and human unity as essential to true compassion. Compassion is not pity (feeling sorry for someone condescendingly) but an awareness of togetherness, a shifting of the relational patterns from domination to communion; it is not sentimentalism (which Anne Douglas defines as "the political sense obfuscated or gone rancid") but doing works of mercy, making justice, and moving toward equality. Compassion is not private (a narcissistic indulgence in egocentricity, an act of self-righteous origins) but must become public and political. It cannot be reduced to mere personalism (the ego feeling we sometimes find in psychological movements today) but is the experience of being caught up in "the pathos of God"—Abraham Herschel's insight that God suffers when man suffers, that he identifies himself with the misery of humanity, and that the believer suffers this pain with God. Finally compassion is not a response to a moral commandment by doing acts of altruism, but a flow of the fullest human and divine energies which issue in the simultaneity of self-love and other-love, grounded in the intuitive sense that self and other are part of a greater unity. Such is the nature of compassion.[14]

It is important that we recognize that what we are developing here is a vision of *faith.* Faith is a gift, but it is also a decision, and this decision for faith involves our capacity to choose optimism, to affirm meaning when it is not obvious, indeed even when it is deftly hidden. We are free, we must choose love, our movement toward compassion is voluntary. Clearly there is the distinct possibility that our generation will not choose love, that we will wrap humanity in a shroud and forfeit this magnificence to a cosmic grave. The evidence is everywhere: the extrapolation of lethal weaponry in a renewed arms race and the dealing of these weapons around the globe in an effort to shore up what our government and others refer to as "national security interests";[15] a renewed sense of *private* futures, isolating individuals from communities, and separating interest groups from concern for a common good; and a return to nationalistic chauvinism.

What is particularly disheartening, even to one gripped with the faith vision of grace and reconciliation we've described here, and eager to translate that enthusiasm into action, is the lack of hope for a new society and a new world order, which one encounters almost everywhere. This lack of hope brings with it a hardness of heart, a growing indifference, which escapes any participation in the struggle for peace and justice. It may be true that an earlier optimism was too naive, both about the psychology of individuals and the autonomy and power of institutions. It seems fair to say that expectations for massive change ran too high in the sixties, that issues were not perceived in their complexity, nor did we consider a time frame other than "now." But today we find growing almost the complete opposite of all this: no optimism, no expectation for change, almost no willingness to struggle with the complexity of issues and to commit ourselves to what Berrigan and others refer to as the "long haul."[16]

As Catholics, as scholars and students, as a pluralistic community dedicated to Catholic higher education and the values and ideals of the Society of Jesus, we are called by our tradition, by the events and circumstances of this moment in human history, and by our unique responsibility to the future, to take up the challenge of Pope John Paul II when he spoke in Hiroshima, pleading for humanity to make a "moral about-face."

> Can we remain passive when we are told that humanity spends
> immensely more money on arms than on development, and when we
> learn that one soldier's equipment costs many times more than a child's
> education? . . . Peace or the survival of the human race is henceforth
> linked indissolubly with progress, development and dignity for all
> people. I urge all scientists, centers of research and universities to study
> more deeply the ethical problems of the technological society. It is a
> question that is closely connected with the problem of the just sharing
> of resources, the use of techniques for peaceful purposes, the
> development of nations.[17]

These words of Pope John Paul II are among the most recent expressions of a revolutionary papal social teaching, more bold in its analysis and more impassioned in its urgency. The modern social teaching of the Magisterium began with Pope Leo XIII's encyclical *Rerum Novarum* (1891), which called for the right to a just wage, including the right to strike when negotiations and arbitration for just wages failed. Leo's concern was picked up by Pius XI in *Quadragesimo Anno* (1931). The lack of concern for employees' welfare and an overcommitment to profit and power were among the themes that he addressed. John XXIII built on this tradition in a highly innovative manner. In his encyclical *Mater et Magistra* (1961), the state is recognized as an active agent in promoting human welfare and protecting human rights. In *Pacem in Terris* (1963), published just months before his death, John spells out the content of *human welfare* and *human rights* and says that "he who possesses certain rights has likewise the duty to claim those rights as marks of his dignity."[18] Indeed, "if civil authorities legislate for or allow anything that is contrary to the moral law . . . neither the laws made nor the authorizations granted can be binding on the conscience of the citizens, since we must obey God rather than men."[19]

Pope Paul VI published two important social documents: an encyclical, *Populorum Progressio* (1967), and an apostolic letter, *Octogesima Adveniens,* published in 1971 to celebrate the eightieth anniversary of Leo's *Rerum Novarum.* Pope Paul calls for "solidarity in action at this turning point in human history" particularly among "those peoples who are striving to escape from hunger, misery, endemic diseases and ignorance . . . those who are looking for a wider share in the benefits of civilization."[20] Paul's letters were termed "warmed-over Marxism" by *The Wall Street Journal* because of statements like these: "The world is given to all, and not only to the rich. That is, private property does not constitute for anyone an absolute and unconditional right."[21] "When so many people are hungry, when so many families suffer from destitution, when so many remain steeped in ignorance, when so many schools, hospitals, and homes worthy of the name remain to be built, all public or private squandering of wealth, all expenditure prompted by motives of national or personal ostentation, every exhausting armaments race becomes an intolerable scandal."[22]

The present Pope has, by anyone's standards, become a globe-trotting evangelist for peace and justice. In his journey to Mexico in 1979, his speeches in Brazil last July, and his recent visit to the Philippines and Japan, he has dramatically lifted up the need for a thoroughgoing restructuring of the world order. These are his words:

> God wants us to be responsible for each other. [He wants] an authentic commitment to our brothers, especially the poorest and most needy, and to a transformation of society.[23]

11

It is difficult to ignore this body of Magisterial teachings, developed over these past twenty years. It is more likely that we will be intimidated by these statements, responding either defensively or with debilitating guilt. But why should we be defensive? Why should we feel guilty? If we locate these teachings in the broader development that I've presented here today—that is, as part of the renewal of Christian faith in a creation-centered theology of grace, reconciliation, and eschatological hope, and as tied to the Church's attempt to recover a sense of mission to the world—perhaps we can simply see these teachings as helpful to us in developing a more precise self-understanding as a Catholic, Jesuit university today.

In his commencement address in the spring of 1980, Father William McInnes, S.J., discussed the notion of service as something that is at the heart of Jesuit education. I think his comments on that occasion should be recalled as we experience this symposium and as we grapple with ways in which to integrate the values of faith and justice with our university life:

> Service does not mean helping others; it means living for others. It recognizes that fullness of life is found not in self-aggrandizement or acquisition, not in power, popularity, or pleasure, but in giving oneself to one's neighbor and to God. It is not just doing good for others whenever I feel like it. Rather it is recognizing that unless I learn to serve others, I will never fully become myself. Service is not a passing sentiment; it's a habitual conviction. Service is the raw material of justice—giving others what is their due. It is the foundation of love, giving to others what is my own. In a world of religious illiteracy, it is a major gateway to faith.[24]

What I am suggesting here is this: that service becomes all that Father McInnes suggests it is only when we add to its generous spirit the spirit of critical analysis and courageous moral action. Archbishop Oscar Romero of El Salvador combined these themes in one of his last sermons to his people before he was assassinated: "We need Christians who are active, critical; who analyze things, who don't accept everything; who know how to say *yes* to justice and *no* to injustice."[25] I would hope that this generation of Loyola students could look back years hence and say, "I learned to be that kind of Christian at Loyola in the eighties."

Notes

1. *Sojourners* 10, No. 2 (February 1981): 20-21.

2. The literature detailing and elaborating this approach to Christian faith in Christ's resurrection is legion. In addition to the major works by theologians like Teilhard, Rahner, Küng, Schillebeeckx, Moltmann, and Metz, all of which are referred to later in this text and subsequent notes, see the more popular works by H. A. Williams, *True Resurrection* (New York: Harper & Row, 1972); G. G. O'Collins, *What They Are Saying About the Resurrection* (New York: Paulist, 1978); and John Shea, *The Challenge of Jesus* (Chicago: Thomas More, 1975); *Stories of God: An Unauthorized Biography* (Chicago: Thomas More, 1978); and *Stories of Faith* (Chicago: Thomas More, 1980). An excellent treatment of current thinking in the area of biblical hermeneutics on this topic is Paul Ricouer, *Essays on Biblical Interpretation,* ed. Lewis Mudge (Philadelphia: Fortress, 1980).

3. This is the approach, for instance, of Daniel Maguire in his new book, *A New American Justice* (New York: Doubleday, 1980).

4. For a comprehensive discussion of this new theology of grace, see Roger Haight, *The Experience and Language of Grace* (New York: Paulist, 1979), and Leonardo Boff, *Liberating Grace* (Maryknoll, N.Y.: Orbis, 1979). See also the very fine symposium papers: Leo J. O'Donovan, "Making Heaven and Earth: Catholic Theology's Search for a Unified View of Nature and History," in *Theology and Discovery: Essays in Honor of Karl Rahner,* ed. William J. Kelly (Milwaukee: Marquette University Press, 1980); and Beatrice Bruteau, "Freedom: If Anyone Is in Christ, That Person Is a New Creation," in *Who Do People Say I Am?,* ed. Francis A. Eigo (Villanova, Pa.: Villanova University Press, 1980), pp. 123-146.

5. See Boff, *Liberating Grace,* pp. 12-13.

6. Rahner's whole theology is a theology of grace, and thus references to his thought on grace are found throughout his enormous corpus. See *Foundations of Christian Faith* (New York: Seabury, 1978), especially pp. 24-89, 116-137. Excellent secondary sources for Rahner's thought include *A World of Grace,* ed. Leo J. O'Donovan (New York: Paulist, 1979) and Louis Roberts, *The Achievement of Karl Rahner* (New York: Herder & Herder, 1967).

7. Teilhard's major theological writings include especially *The Divine Milieu* (New York: Harper & Row, 1960); *The Future of Man* (New York: Harper & Row, 1960), and *Hymn of the Universe* (New York: Harper & Row, 1961).

8. Hans Küng, *On Being a Christian* (New York: Doubleday, 1976), pp. 601-602.

9. Edward Schillebeeckx, *Christ: The Experience of Jesus as Lord* (New York: Seabury, 1980), pp. 638-643.

10. Ibid., p. 514.

11. The literature produced by this new theological movement is voluminous. Some important works by Jürgen Moltmann are: *Theology of Hope* (New York: Harper & Row, 1965); "Political Theology," *Theology Today* 27 (1971): 6-23; "Politics and the Practice of Hope," *Christian Century* 87 (1970): 288-291; and *The Crucified God* (New York: Harper & Row, 1974). J. B. Metz has produced two important articles in English: "Religion and Society in the Light of a Political Theology," *Harvard Theological Review* 61 (1968): 508-522; and "Political Theology," in *Sacramentum Mundi* (New York: Herder & Herder, 1969), 5:34-38. His best English titles are: *Theology of the World* (New York: Herder & Herder, 1969); *Followers of Christ* (New York: Seabury, 1978), and *Faith in History and Society* (New York: Seabury, 1980). See also two more popular books: James McGinnis, *Bread and Justice: Toward a New International Economic Order* (New York: Paulist, 1979); and Gerald Mische and Patricia Mische, *Toward a Human World Order* (New York: Paulist, 1977).

12. Metz, "Religion and Society," p. 513.

13. Ibid., pp. 517-518.

14. See Matthew Fox, *A Spirituality Named Compassion* (Minneapolis: Winston Press, 1979), pp. 1-35.

15. See Richard Barnett, *The Roots of War* (New York: Penguin, 1972) and Mische and Mische, *Toward a Human World Order.*

16. Daniel Berrigan, *Ten Commandments for the Long Haul* (Nashville: Abingdon, 1981).

17. As quoted in the *National Catholic Reporter,* 6 March 1981, p. 21.

18. *Pacem in Terris* (New York: Paulist, 1963), p. 18.

19. Ibid., p. 21.

20. *Populorum Progressio* ("On the Development of Peoples") (United States Catholic Conference, 1967), p. 3.

21. Ibid., p. 18.

22. Ibid., p. 38.

23. As quoted in Penny Lernoux, *Cry of the People* (New York: Doubleday, 1980), pp. 426-427.

24. Rev. William McInnes, S.J., "A Decade of Service," (Commencement address delivered at Loyola University, Chicago, Illinois, May 24, 1980).

25. As quoted in Mary Luke Tobin, *Hope Is an Open Door* (Nashville: Abingdon, 1981), p. 136.

An Analysis of What the "Faith" Element Should Be in "Faith and Justice"

A Response by Francis L. Filas, S.J.

May I first briefly comment that speaking as one strongly influenced by Aristotle, Augustine, and Aquinas, I am in agreement with the ethical conclusions proposed in Dr. Ludwig's thought-provoking paper, and this despite the fact that these conclusions were presented as originating apparently outside such traditional influences. I must place myself with the blind men from Hindustan, who variously felt the elephant and who came away with vastly different opinions as to their palpation, depending on what part of the elephant they felt. Each seemed to be describing a totally different elephant. So it appears am I.

I consider that all the good elements in the highly desirable ethical goals Dr. Ludwig mentioned are but a logical outgrowth from the Church of Jerusalem through and because of the Church of Augustine, through and because of the Church of Trent, and through and because of the Church of the Second Vatican Council. There is no radical break with the past in that Council. If anything, Vatican II made continuity its theme, as for example in paragraph 4 of "The Church in the Modern World": "Very many of our contemporaries are kept from accurately identifying permanent values and adjusting them properly to fresh discoveries."

I also believe that the Greatest Mind of the Western Church is hardly to be classified with Skinner or Wilson. Augustine's Christianity was a living, transcendental organism, not something boxed-in. To my mind vastly differing impressions of Augustine can be obtained, dependent on which Augustine in isolation one reads. When he is contesting one or other adversary, he might appear as Manichean or Pelagian, Monophysite or Nestorian, merciful or rigorous, unfeeling or affectionate, fossilized ancient or adaptable contemporary.

I am uneasy about any ethical outlook that tends to identify a specific political stance as automatically the only moral stance possible. On my part it is not merely a reluctance to brand the policies of the Reagan administration as against minorities as such, or less than favorable to human rights as such. Something so contemporary as the extremely volatile changes on the El Salvador scene might be utterly reversed by the time these lines are read. Various American church groups and Roman Catholic religious superiors have been on the verge of putting the mantle of their ethical approval on the guerilla movement in El Salvador, ready to condemn the United States's political administration for a supposedly immoral decision in not supporting the guerillas. It should be no secret that word came to these religious leaders from El Salvador that the issues were not that simplistic. In March 1981 the Roman Catholic archbishop of San Salvador publicly withdrew his support from the guerilla movement. The conclusion should be self-evident.

While I am in accord with every moral viewpoint that centers on creation as a stepping stone to the Creator, I cannot accept approaches that tend to obscure the distinction between the natural and the supernatural—a distinction that is necessary to God's giving us Jesus Christ freely, and necessary for our free acceptance of this gift.

Truly Christianity in its essence does not cry out that we are depraved, but that we are deprived, and only the freely given and healing grace of Jesus the Redeemer saves us. What is redemption if not redemption from sin? I quote no less than one of the greatest woman geniuses and saints in history, St. Teresa of Avila: "I have a zoo of wild animals in my head."

Newly proposed systems of philosophy and of theology might have differing terms to express their concepts, but they must of necessity face the same reality even if this reality is evolving into new qualities. Reality does not die, reality does not cease to exist, no matter what you call it or where you place it, whether in actual things existing or in mental constructs. Any system that does not come to grips with the daily reality in which we live must dissolve into empty jargon. No system can overcome the impossibility of categorizing the action of the divine. God escapes all categories.

In discussion like our present symposium it seems to be the rule that speakers give primary attention to what is a concrete application of something that they presume is faith-oriented. Therein lies a problem. Only too often a subjective sincerity has been accepted as synonymous with truth. In the name of faith all sorts of excesses have occurred historically. The terms *religious fanatic* and *fiery Savonarola* and *fire-breathing crusader* are too entrenched in our vocabulary to be without foundation. We are confronted with the common human failing of placing God on our side. A diametrically opposite attitude should be there instead: are we placing ourselves on God's side? In all honesty we must ask: how can one be reasonably sure that he or she is on God's side? How does one objectively determine, as far as is humanly possible, what are the valid *faith* foundations for works of justice?

The answer is extremely complex, because it calls for many nuances and distinctions. Before we approach it directly, I should like to insert what might appear as a digression but is actually a biblical application of our basic inquiry: the relationship of faith to justice. This application occurs in the dichotomy that was popularized universally by both sides at the time of the Protestant Reformation: the supposed exclusivity of faith versus good works.

This supposed dichotomy was claimed to exist between the accepted Pauline Epistles, particularly Romans, and the Epistle of James. Paul's polemic was directed against the mechanical observance of the Torah, as if mechanical observance alone were sufficient. But Paul's polemic holds even today. If Paul held that mere Jewish law of itself cannot save, we must hold today that mere Christian law—and mere working for justice—of itself cannot save. The works that James proposes are not those of religious observance, but those of social justice, to remedy social inequities. The works of religious observance that Paul appears to condemn are not, therefore, the social works that James encourages. That historical controversy should never have existed, nor should the sides have appealed to Paul or James as their respective champions. For the works of justice that James urges cannot be carried out ethically if we do not have the objective and properly oriented faith that Paul requires in order to prevent our observances from becoming mere sterile formalism.

The word *conservative* should not mean and does not necessarily mean obstinately protecting and maintaining the status quo. Instead, it means a dipping back into traditional and perennial values in order to adjust to new changes, new technologies, and new challenges.

Therefore I am dipping back into the perennial philosophy of Thomas Aquinas, even farther back into ethical and psychological directions from Aristotle, when I suggest the following norms to answer the question: how does one objectively and correctly determine the validity of faith foundations for some work of justice? I do not presume to have the competence to gauge these norms in the order of true importance.

FIRST: When we approach the likelihood of involvement, it would seem that we should honestly try to determine whether we have an emotional or intellectual bias that would tend to cloud an objective decision, standing of itself. Horace the Roman poet has a wonderful line in this regard: *Mutato nomine, de te fabula narratur.* "Just change the name, and the story is about you."

SECOND: It would appear reasonable to consider the opinions of others who are apparently sober in their awareness of the truth of a situation. The opinions of others are not necessarily correct, but we ought to do more than go through the motions of asking, what have other presumably sound-thinking men and women said and done about this, and why? I emphasize most strongly that while taking stock we should not give up the courage of our own insights merely because they differ from the supposed current attitude.

THIRD: In looking to the past, we should consider the biblical and church teachings not only of our own religious commitment but in the spirit of ecumenical respect of the commitments of others as well. There might exist here morsels of truth otherwise overlooked.

FOURTH: I subscribe to an objective norm of right and wrong, and I uphold the preeminence of conscience as it earnestly and perhaps laboriously seeks to determine whether it is conformed to that norm of right or wrong. But all centuries of ethical analysis, not just our own, have recognized circumstantial and existential elements as of critical importance in shaping final moral decisions.

In saying this I am referring to the qualities of the queen of virtues, prudence, the virtue the ancients used to call the *auriga virtutum,* "the charioteer of the virtues." Prudence cracks the whip; prudence pulls in the reins. Prudence recognizes that in fields of human values a mathematical judgment is not always easy to come by. In some cases a mathematically certain or exact judgment is not possible. Prudence recognizes that in so-called prudential-judgment situations even a Solomon would be confused when rights conflict with rights. Prudence recognizes that there is no such thing as perfect change, since every new change represents a compromise between a set of new advantages and a set of new problems. Prudence asks: will I ultimately do more good or more harm by my actions? If I destroy a present order of things, am I merely a hell-raiser seeking and getting attention, or creating a vacuum and perhaps hurting innocent persons, or do I have an acceptable substitute to offer? On the other hand, what if I am so cowardly as to remain silent when the very rocks shout out to the skies? If we do not have adequate factual information, then we should not rashly take action as if our judgments exhausted the cup of wisdom. It is prudent to cite the repeated admonitions of Pope John Paul II on more than one continent, that priests and religious should press for the application of ethical principles, but that they should abstain from direct political interference. Direct politics, the Pope has often said, is outside the proper sphere of the Church.

I return to the theme with which I began, self-righteousness. We can feel smug and self-satisfied as we berate the ills of our time, but this would hardly be a complacency to be proud of. I suggest a biblical basis for a humility that does indeed work for justice and for the sake of justice, not for self-satisfaction. Scriptural quotations abound in this regard. The same lips that said, "The zeal of my Father's house has eaten me up," also said, "You casuists! you strain out a gnat, and you swallow a camel." Those same lips reprimanded the traitor who covered up his treachery with the callous words, "This could have been sold and given to the poor."

Humbly then we can bring to others not just ourselves with our failings and deficiencies, but rather the grace and goodness of God in ourselves, as we strive to give to them the respect and justice that is due them as imaged creatures of the Lord God.

MINISESSION A

Sister Rita Stalzer, C.S.J.: Our speaker today is new to Loyola, having come in September 1980 as the rector of the Jesuit Community. Father Gerald Grosh entered the Society of Jesus in 1956. In 1972 he received a Ph.D. degree in theology from Fordham University, concentrating on the areas of spirituality, psychiatry and religion, and religious experience. From 1972 to 1978, Father Grosh was a part-time teacher in theology at Xavier University and was extensively involved in pastoral ministry in Cincinnati, Ohio. His ministry has spanned the spectrum of the Church. He has worked with high-school students, college students, married couples, members of religious orders (both women and men), seminarians, and priests. He helped begin Marriage Encounter in Cincinnati. He helped found the Jesuit Renewal Center in Milford and was on that staff from its beginning. He was in charge of the directed retreat ministry at the Center and served as supervisor or director of the various training programs in spiritual direction at the Center. In 1979 he was appointed the director of the Jesuit Renewal Center. Father Grosh spent the year 1975-1976 living among the poor in South America. He taught for three years in the lay pastoral ministry program. He has given numerous talks and published articles in the area of spirituality.

It is my pleasure now to present Father Gerald Grosh.

Psychological and Spiritual Maturity
Necessary for Effecting Justice
Father Gerald R. Grosh, S.J.

I have some definite presuppositions that I have no intention of trying to prove or to justify. I appeal to twelve years of rich pastoral experience of relating deeply with Christians who were eager to grow in their relationship with God and willing to face the pain involved. I appeal to my own life of taking seriously my own spiritual and psychological development. And finally I appeal to your life *if* you have been taking your experience seriously.

I am not going to justify my presuppositions, because I could spend all my time doing that, and we would never address the real issue. The matter is too important to do that. So I am going to presume that you have experience and recognize the validity of my presuppositions.

What are these presuppositions? First of all I am a man of faith. I believe in God's ongoing revelation, that he is always striving to communicate himself to us, that he is always reaching out to us in love. I believe that God is infinite so that there is always more of himself that he wants to share with us. I believe that God communicates with each individual according to his or her capacities. I believe that God communicates with each society according to its capacities.

Fundamentally this means that I believe in development, in the process of human growth. Though I recognize the value of laws, norms, and ideals, I understand them as guidelines and as goals rather than as the reality which is actualized in any given moment of an individual's life. Often enough laws, norms, and ideals lead to a subtle perfectionism and a false guilt which has little to do with the ongoing experience of God's love or the reality of becoming human in the image of Jesus. Finally I believe that the norm of human behavior is the life of Jesus, i.e., that in becoming human we become divine.

These are my presuppositions. I find them in accord with the Gospel, with my own experience, and with the experience of many other Christians. However, I do not believe that this is the way the Christian faith has been formulated or taught by all theologians, nor do I believe that it is the way it has been lived by many who wanted to live a Christian life. At the heart of my presuppositions is the belief in development. Various theories of development help us to understand our experience. I am going to present three that I find most helpful. I think they will shed light on why it is so difficult for American Christians to respond effectively to the call of justice. The theories I will use are those of Kierkegaard, Erikson, and Ignatius.

First let me present Erikson. Erikson describes eight stages in the development of the human person. The most frequently discussed are the fifth, sixth, and seventh stages (identity, intimacy, and generativity). There are two important aspects of his theory: (1) personal development is epigenetic, i.e., each stage builds upon an earlier stage and deepens it; and (2) at each new stage of development there is a crisis, some form of inner conflict; in religious terms we would refer to this as part of the Paschal mystery.

Erikson's fifth stage is identity. This is the sense of self-acceptance that Carl Rogers speaks of. The person can say, "I am good." This usually happens sometime between the ages of twelve and thirty. I recognize that I have a role to play in life. The crisis is precipitated by my having to choose to be someone. Up to this time my image of myself has been what others think of me. Now I choose who I want to be, although even then, once I get my act together, I still need others to affirm it. At this stage of development, the earlier stages are thus integrated: (1) trust (I can accept myself and others); (2) autonomy (I can stand apart and say *yes* without shame); (3) initiative (I can try new things without guilt and use my imagination creatively); and (4) industry (I feel that I have a contribution to make, and I can cooperate with others).

I would also like to comment briefly on the sixth and seventh stages. The crisis of intimacy usually occurs between the ages of twenty-one and thirty-five. Once I feel okay about myself and myself in a group, I still need one person to show my best things to and to share my weaknesses and powerlessness with. I am able to risk my identity without fear of being swallowed up by the other. I can love and allow myself to be loved. I am able to commit myself to another; until I do so, I am still an adolescent. The fact that a person has taken vows of marriage or celibacy does not necessarily imply that the person has gone through this crisis. Many are stagnated at an earlier stage and never do really commit themselves.

The seventh stage, the crisis of generativity, usually occurs between the ages of thirty-five and sixty-five. Here one's focus is outward toward the larger group. I am concerned with establishing and guiding the next generation. I am able to care and to be creative. My concern is the other. I am in possession of myself, I can share, I can give my skills away. The fifth stage (identity) focuses on self; the sixth and seventh stages focus on others or on relationship.

Certain things to be said about Erikson's theory are pertinent to the ability of Americans to effect justice. The present analysis of our American culture concludes that most Americans do not have the basic sense of identity (the fifth stage). They struggle to accept themselves, burdened heavily with a negative self-image. My thesis is this: it takes a generative person, one who has reached the seventh stage of development, to effect justice in our American society. I will try to establish this later, but you can see the direction in which I am heading.

Now I want to talk about Kierkegaard, who presents three levels of growth: the instinctive level, the moral-ethical level, and the level of religious faith.

On the instinctive level the motivation for behavior is the seeking of pleasure and the avoidance of pain. One chooses by his likes and dislikes, by his hopes and fears. The person is very self-centered. Ordinarily he will observe a law literally or else break it. He settles problems by recourse to an outside authority rather than to his own inner judgments.

On the moral-ethical level the motivation for behavior is the keeping of the law. This law may be external and objective (the social order), internal (one's subjective conscience), or a combination of the two (the subjective appropriation of what is valid objectively). When the law is external and objective, it is clear-cut and absolute. What is right is right; what is wrong is wrong. This is determined by one's external authority (church, country, parents, teachers). When the law is internal, the person recognizes the ambiguity of circumstances and personalities. What is right for me may not be right for others; what is right for them may not be right for me. I decide for myself what is right and what is wrong. When my conscience and the objective law mesh, then my conscience is formed in accord with well-chosen principles such as justice, equality of all, or the dignity of the human person.

The person who lives on the moral-ethical level is the person of principle. If he has achieved some internalization of the law, he is a very good person. He represents the best of a liberal education. However, the thesis that I am presenting is that in today's world this person is not mature enough to effect justice. The ultimate values of this person are what is right and what is true. The problem for this person is distinguishing among various rights and various truths. Justice for one person is not necessarily justice for another person. Respecting one person's legal rights is not always respecting another person's legal rights. The person of principle lacks a criterion for adjudicating among legitimate rights.

This brings us to Kierkegaard's third level of development, the level of religious faith. This is the level of personal relationship. The motivation for one's behavior is no longer keeping the law or doing what is right; the motivation is relationship to a person. For the Christian the motivation is relationship to Jesus.

I believe that we have to see this third level, the level of religious faith, in a developmental context. James Fowler has done some work on this. So too have St. Teresa and St. John of the Cross. I find the *Spiritual Exercises* of St. Ignatius most helpful in this context.

Let me say a few things about the *Spiritual Exercises* of St. Ignatius. They are the product of St. Ignatius' own spiritual experience. He set up a structure to help spiritual guides in their helping of individuals in their relationship with God. The *Exercises* were meant for the director and not for the retreatant—to help the director in recognizing the spiritual experience the retreatant is going through. They also present the director with some norms and with some possible ways of facilitating growth in relationship with God.

The focus of the *Spiritual Exercises* is experiential, i.e., the focus is on the real relationship in the *now* moment between the individual and God. What do I mean? We can relate to God as impersonal, or as Father, or as Son, or as the human Jesus, or as the Spirit, and so on. So too the individual person changes. In the present moment, I am who I am, with my present feelings, hopes, and desires, at my own particular stage of psychological and spiritual development. A person's spiritual development is recognized by the person's deepest spiritual desires. Ignatius put these in his Second Prelude; he put them in the form of a grace to be desired. These desires arise naturally within the person as one's spiritual experience happens and grows. A spiritual guide is very helpful in recognizing and facilitating this recognition and the process of growth.

Now let us move through the stages of spiritual development, using the *Spiritual Exercises* as a backdrop. First of all it is important to note that some are not ready to make the *Spiritual Exercises.* Such people have an idealized self-image or a negative self-image. They do not have a personal relationship with the real God. Their God is the God of philosophy. God is the Good or the Truth; he is Judge and Lawgiver. He presents the person with a series of *oughts,* which the person is unable to measure up to. Thus the individual is confronted with a good deal of perfectionism and guilt. A person at this level of development responds to justice as an *ought*; he focuses on the individual's rights and is tinged by guilt at his inability to bring about effective justice. He also tends to lay guilt trips on others. This person is at Kierkegaard's second level of development, the moral-ethical level, or perhaps even at the instinctive level.

A person who is ready to make the *Spiritual Exercises* is a person who is facing self-acceptance. The deepest desire within the person is the desire to be loved for who he or she is. The person's focus is on a healthy sense of self. The person is receptive and passive before the experience of being loved. The person is dealing with becoming a self. This corresponds to the identity stage of Erikson's theory.

There are two stages to the claiming of identity: (1) the acceptance of oneself as good and loved; and (2) the acceptance of oneself as a loved sinner. In accepting the positive side of oneself, one accepts his talents, family, relationships. The image of God is that of a Creator or of a loving Father. One feels himself as being loved as he is. He has a sense of praise, gratitude, and awe, and is filled with life; he recognizes the goodness of himself, others, the world, and God. In accepting the negative dimension of oneself, the person acknowledges being human and sinful. He realizes that he is loved in his sinfulness and that this love is unearned. His image of God is that of Savior, Healer, and Forgiver. When a person has a sense of his own identity, his motivation for justice is a universal ideal such as equality, or brotherhood and sisterhood. He possesses a vague sense of his own identification with all men and women, which extends to his being one with them in his sinfulness. He is able to claim his own part in creating injustice in the world and is truly sorrowful.

The next stage of spiritual development deals with the ability of the person to go out to others, to offer himself to others, to commit himself and invest himself. Here again there are two stages, the interpersonal and the societal. These correspond to Erikson's intimacy and generativity stages. At the interpersonal level, the person offers his gifts and talents (who he is) to a few significant others. He is able too to share his weaknesses, humanity, and vulnerability with them. This is a hesitant and risky venture; but love calls him to do it, and he is willing to respond. The person's image of God is that of the human Jesus, who has saved him from sin and now calls him into intimate friendship with himself. A person at this stage of development tends to confront the issues of injustice through involvement on the local scene. His heart is touched by a personal knowledge of those who are suffering.

196943

At the generative level one faces the cost of discipleship and chooses a self-sacrificing love. One chooses to let go one's own needs for the sake of others. The person desires to follow Jesus; the person knows that following Jesus means following him to death. Usually this involves humiliation, misunderstanding, a sense of betrayal, and the loneliness involved in making a choice. The person's concern for others reaches beyond an interpersonal caring for a few to asking the hard questions about larger issues. The person is concerned for the future; he strives to work for the change of those social, political, and economic structures that foster an unjust world. He strives for compassion rather than a "kindness" that avoids the truth. A generative person embodies the essence of Christian morality in which one loves not just in proportion to another's due (justice) but in proportion to another's needs regardless of the cost to oneself. What I am saying is this: it is this kind of loving, this kind of morality, this stage of psychological and spiritual development, that is necessary in American society if true justice is to be achieved.

Let me review again the stages of spiritual and psychological development and show how justice surfaces at each stage. For the person of principle, justice is what is right or what ought to be done. Usually the person of principle is an angry person. He tends to be defensive and will rationalize his own behavior. He often feels guilt himself when he acts or talks; he is also prone to lay guilt trips on others. His motivation is external, i.e., his *oughts* come from outside himself. He is often a kind person, but he is not really compassionate. He can get wrapped up in causes and fight angrily for what he thinks is right.

When a person is dealing with his own self-acceptance, his focus is more on himself than on what he does for others. Because he experiences himself as loved and blessed by his Father and Creator, he has some sense of unity with men and women throughout the world. He often has a vague sense of identification with the poor and the oppressed. Being a good person, he is frequently confused as to what he should do when he is confronted with injustice. If he is not aware of his own sinfulness, then he tends to be naively optimistic and may join a particular cause, e.g., the peace movement. If he is aware of his own sinfulness, then he generally feels powerless in the face of injustice. He can also accept his own sinfulness with regard to injustice (e.g., environment, economy, multinational corporations) without being defensive.

The person dealing with intimacy, when confronted with injustice, gets involved locally with a few people. Moved deeply by pain and suffering, he is able to sacrifice personally in little ways. He tends to have a Band-Aid approach to immediate needs and suffering. The person who is generative is able to ask the hard questions. He sacrifices beyond his own personal time and energy. He can let go his own culture and economy. He looks at the social structures that create or help foster poverty and unjust oppression and is willing to pay the price of working toward changing these structures.

Why do I say that it is this latter stage of development that is necessary for effecting justice in today's world? Commitment to justice involves: (1) admission that I have sinned personally and through my culture; (2) a willingness to let go my own rights because of the needs and rights of others; and (3) a willingness to accept the criticism of others, who because of their own fears, hurts, and insecurity will not understand my behavior and in fact will judge it as a betrayal of them. Thus behavior that embodies justice calls for a person who is generative (Erikson's seventh stage) and is committed to suffering love (Ignatius's Third Week of the *Spiritual Exercises*). A key factor in the lack of effective involvement in justice is the fact that we have not grown into the psychological and spiritual freedom that is necessary for this kind of commitment.

Discussion

Member of the audience: Your approach seems to highlight the role of feeling and leave little place for the intelligence. Is there any role for the intelligence?

Father Grosh: Yes, the way I would interpret the use of intelligence with regard to effecting justice is very much the way that Bob Ludwig used social analysis in the first presentation today. In other words, one uses one's intelligence to look at the objective phenomena, to look at the world around him or her *beyond the local situation*. If I am going to look at justice in the world today, I can't measure it only by what is right within our American culture.

I have to look at the interrelationships—international relationships—even in terms of the activities here in the United States. So I would see the use of intelligence especially aimed toward social analysis. There is another dimension of intelligence that is operative, though I am not sure whether your question was aimed in this direction. I find the person of principle a very intelligent person; he is always giving reasons. Usually a denial of affect is involved in maintaining those reasons. In my experience I have found that persons of principle rationalize a good deal. They tend to reason logically from truths and to deny the experiential basis. I don't want to deny the use of the critical faculty of intelligence. It is a tremendous gift, but I'm aware that it can be misused, and frankly I think it is misused.

Member of the audience: It seems to me that the academic setting can militate against a developmental approach to education, which is more personalized simply because of the need to impart information. Do you have any ideas on that?

Father Grosh: Yes. I created another institution, or rather I helped create another institution at one point in time. It was an alternative educational institution. I also functioned within an educational institution, but created an educational program different from the strictly cognitive program. Jesuit education has always been flexible and striven to educate the whole person. Some classroom situations are strictly cognitive. This has its strengths as well as its weaknesses. I think, though, that more and more education is looking towards other dimensions of our personality and recognizing them. The Institute of Pastoral Studies is a good example of another form of educational program that is valid.

Member of the audience: Don't you think that the university should provide opportunities for us to address justice issues in a very practical fashion within the university?

Father Grosh: Yes. I would say this symposium is one example of doing this. Actually, the other paper that I proposed for this symposium was on that topic. It didn't get accepted. I'm happy to give this one.

Member of the audience: Do you believe that Christians today are really motivated by a desire to follow Jesus and to share his Passion with him? That's what you are saying, isn't it, that it is only when we are so motivated that we will begin to effect justice?

Father Grosh: Yes, that's what I'm saying. And no, many present-day Christians are not so motivated. But I think the challenge is always there; this is the fundamental call of all Christians. More and more this is being articulated with regard to justice in the present Church. And you know that we fight it. Bob Ludwig gave a long analysis of Church social documents which, if we are really to take them seriously, mean sharing the Paschal mystery. Another dimension was one of the points Father Filas was making, when he talked about the importance of grace. Grace is God's gift. The call to follow Jesus and to share his Paschal mystery is a grace—a gift from God. As much as I talk about development, it is still *God* who calls us to develop. It is *God* who offers us the grace of sharing his Paschal mystery; we do not presume this for ourselves. Now my own belief is that God is preparing us for Paschal mystery living. I gave the *Spiritual Exercises* several years ago to people dealing with an idealized or a negative self-image. They were working through that crisis of growth where the person no longer chooses by fear, but by a sense of being loved as a unique person. I have been with those same people, a couple of years later, when their focus was beginning to move outwards toward love of others. In other words I find these developmental stages happening as part of God's grace, of God's love toward our world.

Member of the audience: Today Kohlberg is saying that there is a stage of moral development beyond his sixth stage.

Father Grosh: Yes, I would see a highly developed person of principle as being a person at Kohlberg's sixth stage. I would want to add a seventh stage of morality—namely, a response to a person. The Christian's motivation for behavior is the following of Christ. It is love for the person of Jesus and a response to his personal call that motivates a Christian to immerse himself in the struggle for justice in our world today.

Member of the audience: It seems to me that a person, no matter what his stage of development, should be concerned about unjust social structures. Why do you identify this concern with Erikson's seventh stage (generativity)?

Father Grosh: That is a legitimate question. Why would I apply the stage of generativity to the changing of social structures? I think I could apply the stage of generativity to many things. I would apply it to the changing of social structures just because of the existing situation in our world today. In this symposium we are talking about the integration of faith and justice. In my own struggle to realize what this means in the practical order in my own life, I have reached two conclusions: (1) all of us Americans are called to live a simple lifestyle and to stop using the peripheral products of our consumeristic society; and (2) all of us are called to work toward the changing of unjust social, economic, and political structures. I see the Church challenging Catholics to this. I see the Society of Jesus challenging Jesuits to this. Let's face it. Many Americans are very comfortable within social, economic, and political structures that create unjust situations for other Americans and for people of other nations. I think it takes a person at the level of generativity to let go his own comfort, and perhaps even his own rights, in order to engage in the struggle for a just world.

MINISESSION B

Mr. Tom Kenemore: Good afternoon and welcome to our session. I would like to introduce you to our presenter, Ms. Mary Kay Kramer, who is connected with Loyola University in a variety of ways. She is a graduate of the School of Social Work and is currently serving on the alumni board as vice-president. She works at the Medical Center in the Social Work Department as a coordinator of the Geriatric Program and the Outreach Community Team. She is serving at the Medical Center as a field instructor for students in the graduate program of the School of Social Work. In

September 1980 she became a parent of a Loyola student; her daughter Katie started attending Lakeshore Campus.

Ms. Kramer will discuss "A Right to Life for the Older Adult." Ms. Kramer.

A Right to Life for the Older Adult
Mary Kay Kramer, M.S.W.

I'm sure you're familiar with the term "a right to life." The pro-life movement promotes the respect for life of the unborn child. President Reagan recently challenged the definition of the dignity of life, asking when life begins for the unborn child. It is without question a strong movement politically, one that focuses on the intrinsic respect and reverence for the dignity of the individual person.

The mystery of the dignity of man for the older adult. If we question when the beginning of life occurs—what about when it ends? At the other end of life's spectrum, near the ending, in the final years, does life fade slowly away? When does a man lose his dignity? Is it when he's told he has to retire? At age sixty or sixty-five, when he's no longer able to continue his employment, his life's achievement, his career? What about a woman—when does she become unworthy of our respect? Is it when the children have all left home and the first wrinkles begin to appear? Or is it when her figure begins to sag and her hair turns gray? Does dignity diminish with false teeth, hearing aids and arthritis? Are these signs—like the color of a man's skin—that say, *You are different; you're less than human; you can be ignored, discounted, devalued, ostracized?*

It's good to know your place. It's okay if you go off and live with your own kind. People over sixty-five can live in retirement villages, not in *our* neighborhood. You who have trouble remembering, who forget details, who get instructions and dates all mixed up. You who use canes or walkers or have fingers and hands that are crippled with rheumatism—you're different—you're not pleasant to look at or to have around. There are places called nursing homes that take care of people like you. It's good to know your place.

When we see you with all the signs of old age, we are reminded that we may become like you some day and that is *the greatest insult* of all, you know. Is it something like being black or being a member of a minority? But worse in a way—you remind us of the imminent termination of our life—death itself. People who don't cherish their elderly have forgotten whence they came and whither they go, suggests Ramsey Clark.

Within the next twenty to forty years, it is predicted that we will witness a geriatric population explosion. From a youth-oriented society, we will experience a major demographic shift to an older-adult-dominated population; that is, the number of senior citizens sixty years of age and older will double. Older adults will have power simply because of their numbers. Naturally this transition will be reflected in our attitudes, our life style, our value system, our ethics. What kind of conflict or adjustment will this transition present in the 1980s?

The older population, with high levels of stress and disability, seek the help of their physicians twice as often, are hospitalized twice as much for twice as long as the younger population. It is mind-boggling to envision the need for physicians, for health and social services, for Medicare and insurance benefits in the next twenty years.

I suggest that this transition will require us to prepare, as individuals and as a nation. Loyola University and Loyola Medical Center can contribute immensely in the area of education and research by exploring this vast and fascinating topic, for instance *the health aspect of aging.*

1. Why do some people develop abnormal manifestations of aging while others do not?

2. What are some of the positive aspects of a healthy aging process?

3. How can Loyola contribute and promote gerontology in a society which historically has neglected and discounted its elderly population?

The solution to some of the problems lies within ourselves. Aging is not a disease but a normal, natural process, which in no way decreases a man's dignity.

But how can we learn to grow old gracefully? If it is true that a man ages as he has lived, then it makes sense that the best preparation for meeting the stress and problems of the declining years may be sound mental health in early life. Every time life asks us to give up a desire, adjust to a new direction, redefine our goals or start a new plan, we are invited to widen our perspectives. Henri J. Nouwen reflects that every time we are jolted by life, we are faced with the need to trust a new pathway, a new beginning. If this doesn't happen in the early years, how can we ever expect that it will come about later in our old age? There is no question that the greatest stress on the human organism is in the last stage of life. Robert Butler suggests that "aging is an intrinsic part of the developmental cycle. Aging has its own problems, strengths, qualifications with the potential for change up to the very end of life."

In looking at life's stages, Erik Erikson presents a theory oriented toward internal dynamics and emphasizes that the developmental tasks have the potential to become the bases for competence and identity in maturity. Situational factors almost always can be found in the history of the aged patient who presents pathological symptoms. The personality structure is challenged by the losses. The attributes that have contributed in life to a man's self-esteem and gratification wane and are depleted in this last phase of the life cycle. How flexible is the personality?

This may be the most difficult time of all to be aging. Change is all-pervasive. The aged person has to withstand the cultural shock of this rapid change in society. Everything that our nation stands for, everything we believe in, all that has sustained us, all we have held dear is being brought into question. Religion, morality, government, ethics, family, marriage, and work habits are all being challenged; all are in the process of change. That is why growing old gracefully requires preparation. Most people don't believe this.

"Aging is the turning of the wheel, the gradual fulfillment of the life cycle in which receiving matures in giving, and living makes dying worthwhile. Aging does not need to be hidden or denied, but can be understood, affirmed, and experienced as a process of growth in which the mystery of life is slowly revealed to us. Without the aged we might forget that we too are aging. The elderly are our prophets; they also remind us that what we see so clearly in them is a process in which we all share [Henri J. Nouwen]."

	Environmental Stress	Losses—Situation Disturbance
Trust	Mistrust	Paranoid State Projection Delusions
Autonomy	Shame, Doubt	Over-dependency Depression Anger-Rage
Industry (Initiative)	Inferiority, Guilt	Low Self-esteem Isolation— Withdrawal
Ego Identity	Role Confusion	Disorientation Sense of Uselessness
Intimacy	Isolation	Recluse—Hermit Narcissistic— Pathology
Generativity	Stagnation	Hypochondriasis Denial
Identity- Integrity	Despair	Severe Depression Alcoholism Behavioral Problems

Discussion

Mr. Kenemore: Mary Kay has three questions that she suggests we use as guides for discussion: (1) What research proposals would you suggest to promote a healthy normal aging process? (2) Why do some people develop abnormal manifestations of aging and others do not? (3) What part does stress play in the aging development process?

Member of the audience: Who is old?

Ms. Kramer: I am including in this talk those sixty years of age and older.

Member of the audience: Are we speaking of psychological aging rather than physical aging?

Ms. Kramer: Father James Mertz in his nineties was told by his doctor that the doctor would like to exchange hearts with him.

Member of the audience: I am presently on my last university contract because I am sixty-five. I personally resent being forced to retire at sixty-five or seventy. That young people are waiting to take over one's job is no reason to have to retire.

Ms. Kramer: I agree with you. In my work I witness people who had never had a depression being hospitalized when they were forced to retire.

Member of the audience: A woman I know died because her daughter insisted on doing too much for her after she retired. The daughter made her into an invalid.

Ms. Kramer: The child made a child of her mother and reversed roles.

Member of the audience: Why do we always react in a negative way to being old?

Ms. Kramer: Any group that is presently thirty-six million strong and will be eighty-four million in a few years, almost half the population, ought to be seen as a normal group.

Member of the audience: I'm delighted that the Loyola Medical Center is looking into this problem. We must begin to find alternatives to present ways of handling the problem of aging. I know a senior citizens' group that was having its Social Security checks stolen. With the aid of the police department they organized a bus program to drive them to a shopping center and give them some protection. With that aid, they have gone on to organize a more complete program on their own. The increase in the number of elderly means an increase in health care costs. What will happen if benefits are cut back? Where will we find the skilled care necessary to care for these people?

Ms. Kramer: A very important point. The need for physicians alone will be tremendous. I don't see many medical students interested in the aged population. Perhaps their first experience in medical school—working with cadavers—is not the right one. Doctors want to heal, mend, be successful. They do not want to be failures.

Member of the audience: Yes, students see the elderly stereotypically. Age itself is the disease, and it can't be cured. How can we modify these attitudes?

Ms. Kramer: The elderly are going to have to see themselves as a political force and work for effective help.

Member of the audience: Is there any solid information on the relative effectiveness of retirement homes in urban and in rural surroundings? I've always heard that if people live in cities all their lives, they are lost if they are moved to the country.

Ms. Kramer: Reactions are individual and frequently unpredictable. Some people from the city retire to Sun City to live. They have their card games and their swimming pool. The weather is lovely, and they love it. But the real problem is that a sector of the population is being segregated. There is no interaction with other age groups in these retirement communities. People in schools live in another world. Possibly segregation is a greater cause of unhappiness among the elderly than the location of their retirement.

Member of the audience: The mention of people in schools reminds me of my newly-married, seventy-three-year-old mother-in-law who is a regular student in a college in New York. The crucial thing for me is not where we should "put" the elderly, but the availability of options and choices for the individual. They may want to be near little kids and lots of noise; they may not. They ought to be able to choose. It is sad that, because we are so ambulatory and our families move around, the traditional interaction of the extended family is no longer possible. I was raised in a family where there were aunts and grandparents; Sunday dinners might include eighteen or nineteen people. Most of my children's friends will not have this experience. It's a great gap in their education.

Ms. Kramer: I agree.

Member of the audience: When I retire I might want to work, and it would be nice if I could. But we must be realistic. If what could be half of the population were to continue to work, younger people who need jobs would not be able to find them. Perhaps volunteering is a better alternative.

Ms. Kramer: I understand the problem that you are raising. But why could not the older, more experienced adult work side-by-side with the younger, perhaps in a consultant or adviser relationship?

Member of the audience: May it not be that the decreasing number of the young will solve the problem? We will need the elderly to help keep society going. Ms. Kramer, what ideas do you have for research in this area?

Ms. Kramer: There is a lot we don't know about the aging process. Stress among our aged population now causes functional disorders that we had not encountered in earlier years. Stress is one of the areas I would like to see explored. One example of stress: our outreach team goes out every two weeks to a nursing home, and it's appalling the way these people are living. There is one little black lady I know. When she was in the hospital, she had been very paranoid. She came in with a little pile of money, the public aid checks that she had been saving. Yet she had been going around in her building, begging door to door for something to eat. She was afraid to go out of her building, and she was a bit crippled with arthritis. Two people had been visiting her in the hospital and claimed to be relatives. One day the secretary on the unit called me aside and said, "Mary Kay, this lady tells me that these people are not her relatives. Don't give them the money." I said, "What do you mean?" "You know, she came in with almost $2,000." Well, I could not believe it. As it happened, on the doctor's recommendation she was placed in a very large nursing home, one that we visited on the outreach team. We made sure the money was safe; it was not turned over to the two "relatives," and they never showed up again. The end of the story is very sad. She just deteriorated over a period of time once she was removed from her familiar setting. About a month ago she passed away, and we found out that those two so-called relatives had moved everything out of her apartment.

The police run into similar cases of stress all the time. There was a case on television where this person said that somebody had broken into her apartment and beaten her up badly, and she had no one to turn to for help. The Department of Family Relations followed through on the case. They really helped her. But after she recovered, she went back to her apartment only to find that it had been ransacked. So she had to be institutionalized for her own safety.

Member of the audience: Perhaps we need more intermediate facilities, like those the Jewish Council for the Elderly has established, small apartments in a larger complex that provides common areas as well. But all these facilities are quite expensive, beyond the reach of many of those who most need them.

Let me share an example of creative thinking. My dad will be ninety-two in a couple of weeks. He's still living where he has lived for the past twenty years. Now he can't see or hear. He can barely walk with the aid of a cane. But he's still independent. He has a support system that comes from a wonderful pilot project we are praying will not be eliminated in future national budget cuts. He has a housekeeper who comes in five days a week for less than half a day each time. One of those days an R.N. comes to check his health and nutrition. Two other days he is picked up by car and taken to a community center. Now no family can handle the whole load. But with this help he can remain in his home where he is very happy in spite of his infirmities.

Day-care centers are another way of handling the problem of the elderly. While the working adults are away during the day, the elderly are well taken care of; at night they are at home with their families.

Mr. Kenemore: We will have to stop now. I would like to thank Mary Kay Kramer for resensitizing us to an issue that is affecting us all at this very moment. Thank you all for coming.

MINISESSION C

Ms. Patricia G. Graham: I would like to welcome you this afternoon to the talk on "Marriage and Family in Search of a Future." Dr. Thomas G. Cunningham will be our speaker. He is an associate professor of theology here at Loyola. He teaches Christian marriage. His degrees are from Catholic University in canon law. He has worked in the ecclesiastical matrimonial courts and has published an article on the law of the dissolution of the matrimonial bond in the Roman Catholic Church from the decretals of Gregory the Ninth in 1234 to the present.

Dr. Cunningham.

Marriage and Family in Search of a Future
Dr. Thomas G. Cunningham

In the 1920s there emerged a hope that contraception would free humankind from inner constraint in regard to sexual activity, and free it from the fear of pregnancy. There was a growing sophistication about what were seen as outmoded moral standards no longer enforceable by state or family. Bertrand Russell expected the younger generation to produce a more humane society. He described the newly emancipated as

> ... freer from priggery, less inhibited, less enslaved to authority devoid of rational foundation. I think also that they are likely to prove less cruel, less brutal, and less violent than their seniors. For it has been characteristic of American life to take out in violence the anarchic impulses which could not find an outlet in sex.[1]

That certainly puts a heavy burden on sex. Walter Lippmann was a little more wary. He pointed out that there already was a generation which had lived without the Puritan or Victorian restraints but that "instead of the gladness which they were promised, they seem . . . to have found the wasteland. . . ."[2] Now, fifty years later, Gay Talese can suggest that sex has no meaning beyond being a simple recreational activity.[3]

On the other hand, enlightenment and sophistication have led some people to such confusion that celibacy has been proposed as the answer, at least until we can begin to make some sense of it all.[4] This is not the celibacy of commitment, but the celibacy of those no longer able to act.

This latter suggestion is reminiscent of the story of the Achilpa tribe, a nomadic aboriginal group who made their way around by using a pole made from the sacred gum tree as a direction finder. On one occasion a group who had broken their pole and consequently were no longer able to decide on a direction to travel were found sitting down preparing to die.[5] If all directions are of equal worth, how does one choose?

The problem seems to be that we have been unable to move beyond a protest against some outdated standards to the affirming of some positive and humane goals. The fact that external authority can no longer enforce the old conventions is not to suggest that we have no need of conventions. This problem has ramifications beyond marriage itself, but it is particularly pertinent to marriage. Because of the previous tendency of the civil law to enforce certain moral standards, there was confusion about just what morality was all about. The refusal by the state to continue enforcing the laws against certain private actions has led many to assume that this implies approval. To have no publicly enforceable standards simply creates a vacuum, which needs to be filled by the individual or preferably by communities proclaiming inherent values. Freedom from outmoded constraints becomes significant only when it makes it possible for us to be free for something of worth. This, society has not done particularly well. The separation and compartmentalization of the various functions of sex that resulted from the new freedom provoked another warning from Walter Lippmann,

> But if you idealize the logic of birth control, make parenthood a separate vocation, isolate love from work and the hard realities of living, and say that it must be spontaneous and carefree, what have you done? You have separated it from all the important activities which it might stimulate and liberate. You have made love spontaneous but empty, and you have made home-building and parenthood efficient, responsible, and dull.[6]

Fifty years after the warning the fear is being realized. Home-building and parenting are seen by many as dull and limiting; the very institution of marriage is under attack. The contemporary situation is not unlike that faced by Augustine as he formulated a defense of marriage against the Manichees.

The current situation in regard to marriage is very much at odds with the tradition of the West in two respects. First, the biblical tradition presents us with significant conflict between the ideal and the reality. We have stories of lust, polygamy, adultery, murder, incest, told against a background that still preserved a model such as that in Genesis 2:18-24. In the New Testament an attempt is made to restore the ideal of a permanent monogamous union in both the Gospels and Paul.[7] The same tension continues throughout the development of Western theological and pastoral thought. Now there is a tendency to misuse sociological data by measuring what is and stopping there. The new morality becomes identified not with values that challenge us to transcend our present condition, but with the canonization of present practice. A recent book suggests that the wave of the future will be "Successive Polygamy." The reason frequently offered for this is that extended life expectancy makes it highly unlikely that a man and a woman can survive the long relationship of monogamy, and consequently should periodically change partners. This betrays a rather shallow perception of the human person. More importantly it simply states, "If this is what is happening, it must be all right."

The second level on which there is a dramatic break with the past is that of passion. The great stories of love in the West are filled with doomed lovers. As Denis De Rougemont put it,

> Romance only comes into existence where love is fatal, frowned upon and doomed by life itself. What stirs lyrical poets to their finest flights is neither the delight of the senses nor the fruitful contentment of the settled couple: not the satisfaction of love, but its *passion*. And passion means suffering.[8]

The story of Tristan and Iseult becomes the model. Reason does not rule. The lovers are drawn together even though it means suffering and death. This is not to suggest that all lovers must be doomed to die, but rather that passionate commitment will mean being prepared to struggle to overcome difficulties in order to achieve union with the beloved. The present suggestion is that detachment is the answer. We must be able to enter into liaisons without making demands upon each other. "I will love until it begins to hurt." Rollo May suggests that apathy is our present problem and describes it as "want of feeling: lack of passion, emotion or excitement, indifference."[9] The fear of suffering appears to have resulted in the willingness to give up all feeling, even joy. It is interesting to note that the astronauts were chosen because of their ability to withdraw into themselves, remain cool and detached, even while experiencing sensual deprivation for long periods of time.[10]

Any worthwhile comment on the institution of marriage would need to respond to these two deficiencies, i.e., the lack of values that can attract us to transcend our present situation, and the absence of passionate commitment. The two are inextricably interwoven.

In an age that thrives on documentation, it hardly seems necessary to bore the listener with statistics. Even the popular press has bombarded us with a plethora of stories about divorce of husband from wife, of child from parent, of violence in the home, and perhaps among the saddest comments of all, the use of abortion as a contraceptive procedure. A contradiction but a fact. Bertrand Russell had hoped for new generations who would be, "less cruel, less brutal, and less violent than their seniors."[11] The Alan Guttmacher Institute has just reported that in the United States 30 percent of all pregnancies in 1979, between 1,540,000 and 1,600,000, were terminated by abortion. With all the sophistication and freedom from anxiety that seemed to be promised in 1929, a recent United Press International report claims that in 1978 there were 1,100,000 teenage pregnancies resulting in 434,000 abortions. The statistics are staggering and depressing; three women in ten having an abortion have had at least one previous abortion, and 10 percent were not performed until the second trimester. The most common surgical procedure in the United States is abortion. Putting all these statistics together, the Guttmacher Institute suggests we need more abortion clinics. Whatever happened to the new sophistication about birth control? Why are so many unwanted pregnancies taking place? Surely there must be a more humane solution than increasing the number of abortion clinics.

Apart from the statistics, the arts also reflect concern with the condition of the American family. One can look to the classic dramas such as Eugene O'Neill's comment on family life in *Long Day's Journey into Night,* or his story of doomed love and marriage for which he chose the title *The Iceman Cometh,* a line from a dirty joke. Even Hollywood has become serious about these pressures and problems, as reflected in *Alice Doesn't Live Here Anymore, An Unmarried Woman, Interiors, Kramer vs. Kramer, The Great Santini, Breaking Away, Ordinary People.* There is an obvious attempt to do more than entertain and to break through stereotypical presentations of the past and most importantly to leave us with some unanswered question.

One prominent religious response has been that of the Moral Majority, which quite frequently fails to perceive the complexities of life and whose answers are too simple to be convincing. On the other hand, many more liberally-minded religious people have become so overwhelmed by the complexities that they have remained mute in the face of the critical condition of family life. Part of this dilemma can be attributed to the problem of responding to an empirically-oriented society in a nonempirical fashion. We have become so preoccupied with data that we often create the impression that what cannot be digested by a computer does not exist. Even love, so difficult to measure, is frequently replaced by performance that is measurable. In the words of Rollo May,

> It is an old and ironic habit of human beings to run faster when we have lost our way: and we grasp more fiercely at research, statistics and technical aids in sex when we have lost the values and meaning of love. [12]

There is no overwhelming statistical argument to prove that life has meaning. One must at least acknowledge that the evidence is ambiguous. The acknowledgment of this ambiguity should eliminate complacency on the part of the person of faith. However, it does not eliminate faith as an affirmation of the fundamental goodness of it all, of the belief that we are able to transcend the finiteness under which we labor, and to reach out of our isolation. This combination of realism and hope has deep biblical roots. It is the eschatological vision we see in Jesus, who could challenge us to the very core of our being, yet be so understanding and compassionate of the individual sinner. It is the same eschatological vision applied to the field of ethics so well by Reinhold Niebuhr.[13] Not only may we not settle for the worst, but the best we do is challenged by future possibilities. It is this combination of realism and vision that the Christian must keep in balance.

The tendency in dealing with marriage is to begin with marriage itself. It would seem more appropriate to begin with the problems and needs that are common to everyone, whether single and eventually intending marriage, or committed to celibacy for positive reasons, or in the married state. From the myth of the Fall to contemporary psychoanalysis, the terms may change, but humankind is presented as in the world yet somehow isolated and alienated from it and its own kind. This has been the theme of so much of the literature of the postmodern era.

During the sixties a variety of groups within society attempted to overcome that isolation. Haight-Ashbury and its 1967 Summer of Love was one example, but the indiscriminate nature of human closeness, combined with a lack of realism about love's being sufficient for a society, rather quickly ended that experiment. It is not simply human closeness that is needed, but genuine intimacy, and for that intimacy to be genuine, it must be discriminating. This latter quality was certainly one of the missing ingredients. One can only respond to a society in which relationships are often neither discriminating nor responsible by showing that these qualities are not only commendable but possible. Only in this manner can we find in ourselves and encourage in others what Rollo May calls "humane life-giving qualities."[14] This is just as true for the celibate as for the married person, though some modes of expression are different. The concern here, however, is with marriage and specifically marriage seen as Christian sacrament.

Considering the recurring themes of isolation and alienation in contemporary society, something of a miracle is involved when two of whom Paul Tillich calls "the most impenetrable of beings,"[15] move from being total strangers to being willing to risk marital commitment. Each time it happens there is a public involvement, whether we acknowledge it or not. If we can accept marriage as the commitment of a man and a woman to a creative openness to life and mutuality of life, then the commitment is obviously not the achievement. The sign involved then is one of hope, which is realized in varying degrees or unfortunately not at all.

Both failure and success supply ample opportunities for a Christian response. There is joy in the realized hope, which keeps the eschatological vision before the Christian community. But there is also a great opportunity for showing compassion when there is failure. Failure is a reminder of our finiteness and calls for understanding and support rather than condemnation or exclusion from the community. In summary and on a theoretical level, marriage can be described as an act of faith and commitment whereby a man and a woman affirm their belief in the possibility of overcoming their isolation and achieving together in a permanent union a creative openness to and mutuality of life. The Christian community celebrates this event because of its significance for all of us.

Moving from the theoretical to the practical, what can be done to assist the couple in realizing their hope? Our society brings with it its own particular brand of pressures and burdens. Some of these are exacerbated by the loss of the extended family, so that many young couples are called upon to deal with problems without a broad base of support. One unfortunate consequence is that there can be a serious temptation, having just succeeded in opening themselves up to each other, to see themselves as cut off from everyone else. From an isolated self to an isolated couple is a progressive step, but it may not be a tremendous improvement. Not all extended families in the past were indeed a constructive support base for young couples. One can readily see, however, how significant it could be to have such a base. If we are agreed upon that, then we can look for creative alternatives. It would be important to educate young couples so that they do not feel they must depend exclusively on their own resources. I am not suggesting that marriage be open in the manner the O'Neills suggested more than a decade ago. Pointing to the frequent inadequacy of the marital relationship, they suggested opening it up to the possibility of a number of other relationships. To suggest that the problems of one relationship could be resolved by engaging in a number of other relationships is to say no more than that quantity could make up for lack of quality.[16] It would make more sense to expend one's energy, instead, in working to overcome the deficiencies of the original.

Nevertheless, the unique character of the husband-wife relationship has too often been defined by exclusivity. An alternative is that of families not tied by blood relating to each other as families, thereby establishing their own extended unit. This is not a completely original idea. In recent history, a Chicago couple made a great contribution in this area when Mrs. Pat Crowley some years ago decided that the idea of women removing themselves to the kitchen after a dinner party was not acceptable, and eventually the Christian Family Movement was born, in which it was emphasized that couples could and should relate to each other as couples. Indeed they did, and many creative people and things came out of that organization.

There is an idea here that can be built upon. People need to be educated to the possibility of building communities of families. They need not necessarily live together as in a commune. Nevertheless, they should be emotionally and psychologically committed and available to each other. There are various kinds of cooperatives in our society for purposes that range from buying fruit and vegetables to sharing a high-rise. There is a clear need for communities of families who share a common belief in the positive values of marriage and family life and are committed to support each other. The individual family unit can avoid becoming too turned-in upon itself. Mutual support can go a long way toward alleviating many of the pressures child-raising involves.

A second very practical consideration for employing institutions, and this obviously includes Loyola University of Chicago, is to become adaptable to the changing structure of family life. Some changes are the consequence of negative pressures, e.g., financial pressures in an inflationary society, or the very difficult lot of the single parent; but some of them are the result of positive forces at work as women emerge more and more in their own right in society. In the past, women who decided to return to the work force when their children entered grade school were most often limited to part-time jobs and, more importantly, part-time pay in order to be able to see their children off to school and greet them on their return. They were frequently excluded from employment benefits and the possibility of advancement. This area could be addressed by considering shared positions. Not every position lends itself to this, but some do. Instead of the option of either one full-time worker or a number of part-time workers for a position, one could have two persons sharing one full-time spot and arranging their schedules to fit both the employers' and their own family's needs. Some organizations have already tried this, e.g., in one situation two women who are therapists, neither of whom could give full time to agency work, shared a full-time position. I know of at least one situation in which one full-time faculty position was shared by a husband and wife who had small children. This presents some special difficulties because of tenure. Nevertheless, as we find more couples in academic life, some true horror stories are emerging about couples raising a family and having academic positions far removed from each other.

In the final analysis the changed conditions of family life call for society to respond in some creative fashion to the different shape of family needs. Institutions are frequently in a better position than individuals to give direction to these responses. Within the Loyola community there are already clear indications of concern for the condition of marriage and the life of the family. Rollo May suggests, "Life comes from physical survival; the good life comes from what we care about."[17] If it is true of individuals, it is likewise true of institutions. Loyola's pursuit of ways to support family life in these trying times could go a long way toward establishing ethical identity.

Notes

1. Bertrand Russell, *Marriage and Morals* (New York: H. Liveright, 1929), p. 129.

2. Walter Lippmann, *A Preface to Morals* (Boston: Beacon Hill Press, 1929), p. 302.

3. Gay Talese, *Thy Neighbor's Wife* (New York: Doubleday, 1980).

4. Recently discussed on the Phil Donahue Show.

5. Mircea Eliade, *The Sacred and the Profane* (New York: Harper & Row, 1961), p. 33.

6. Lippmann, *Preface to Morals,* p. 290.

7. Mark 10:2-12; Matt. 5:39-32, 19:3-12; Luke 16:18; 1 Cor. 7:10-11.

8. Denis De Rougemont, *Love in the Western World* (New York: Pantheon, 1940), p. 15.

9. Rollo May, *Love and Will* (New York: W. W. Norton & Co., 1969), p. 29.

10. Tom Wolfe, *The Right Stuff* (New York: Farrar, Straus, Giroux, 1979).

11. Russell, p. 129.

12. May, *Love and Will,* p. 15.

13. Reinhold Niebuhr, *An Interpretation of Christian Ethics* (New York: Harper & Brothers, 1935).

14. May, *Love and Will,* p. 63.

15. Paul Tillich, *Love, Power and Justice* (New York: Oxford University Press, 1954), p. 26.

16. Nena O'Neill and George O'Neill, *Open Marriage* (New York: Evans, 1972).

17. May, *Love and Will,* p. 289.

Discussion

Ms. Graham: Thank you very much, Dr. Cunningham, for defining the problems of marriage in our society and for suggesting ways in which we can consider this whole topic of marriage, especially what Loyola needs to do. Are there any questions?

Member of the audience: Is there something special that the twenty-eight Jesuit universities across the country ought to be doing?

Dr. Cunningham: Although we have always taught a course on Christian marriage, we are beginning to realize that marriage is of concern to psychology, psychiatry, sociology, as well as to theology. The theology department is presently trying to work out an interdisciplinary course that would take advantage of the resources of the university and also do justice to all the facets of marriage.

Member of the audience: It's true, isn't it, in your opinion, that we frequently back off once we see the magnitude of any problem?

Dr. Cunningham: That's true. What makes the problem even bigger is that problems of marriage are really not very different from the problems of the single person. How in a dehumanized, technologized society can we help everyone go successfully through all of life's stages so they will be ready for the next stage and not have to experience failure?

Member of the audience: Since marriage is a process, our preparation is never complete, is it? How can we continue to update ourselves and renew ourselves?

Dr. Cunningham: Pannenberg says that what is most distinctive of a human person is openness. The very fact that marriage is a continuing problem insures the need for openness and helps keep life interesting, even exciting.

Member of the audience: There are practical problems we ought to address. What support systems are needed and can the university furnish them?

Dr. Cunningham: A while ago the university established a day-care center. Possibly the motivation was more to help returning women students than it was to help faculty and staff. Presently the center is located at St. Ignatius Parish. What is perhaps even more needed is increased flexibility in the work schedules, as well as more accommodating hours, and nine-month contracts for the staff so that they could be free in the summer.

Member of the audience: It would be helpful if there were.

Member of the audience: What do you see as the main problem in marriages today?

Dr. Cunningham: In marriages there are two sets of relationships, and both must be attended to: the relation of husband and wife and the relation of parents to children. One relationship cannot be used as an excuse to neglect the other.

Member of the audience: Is there not also the problem of two careers within one marriage? Frequently one partner has to be the wage earner while the other goes to school.

Dr. Cunningham: Yes, this is a real problem. Frequently enough, even arrangements agreed to before the problem arises do not turn out to be satisfactory, because the partners did not at the time realize the implications of what they were agreeing to. For example, a couple can agree to being equally available to their children before they have children. It may turn out to be quite difficult and maybe even impossible at times to keep to that agreement.

Member of the audience: The whole role of women in the professions and in business needs a thorough examination.

Dr. Cunningham: I remember a woman who was a Ph.D. candidate in history at Loyola. She was here because a neighboring university refused to have women students after they were forty years of age. But she could not have come to graduate school any earlier because she had been responsible for the day-to-day raising of her children. But things certainly keep changing. When I first came to Loyola there were very few women in my classes; now there are many. So there are new problems because there are greater numbers.

Member of the audience: But beyond these practical problems, must we not also speak of the need to constantly renew the substance of marriage, the love and tenderness one person has for another?

Dr. Cunningham: That's the reason I defined marriage as a commitment of a man and a woman to create an openness to life and a mutuality of life. That's the base from which a marriage must operate. But practical difficulties can become oppressive and difficult to bear. For example, I know two faculty members who have tenure in two different state universities in two different states. They have children. They must make the weekend bear the full weight of providing the love and commitment and mutuality of life that they need.

Ms. Graham: I hope that everyone will attend the reception that is just beginning, and that we can continue the discussion.

SECOND GENERAL SESSION
Dr. Kathleen McCourt
Dr. Kirsten Grønbjerg
Dr. Robert McNamara
Dr. Robert Monks
(from left to right)

Race and Distributive Justice in Chicago: Does Loyola Have a Local Responsibility?

Dr. Kirsten Grønbjerg
Dr. Kathleen McCourt
Dr. Robert McNamara
Department of Sociology

Moderator
Dr. Robert Monks
Director of Continuing Education

Responder
Dr. Murray L. Gruber
School of Social Work

Dr. Monks: It is my pleasure to welcome you to the second general session of the 1981 Loyola-Baumgarth Symposium on Values and Ethics. The topic of discussion this afternoon is "Race and Distributive Justice in Chicago: Does Loyola Have a Local Responsibility?" The paper is by Dr. Kirsten Grønbjerg, Dr. Kathleen McCourt, and Dr. Robert McNamara, all from the Department of Sociology.

Dr. Grønbjerg is a native of Denmark. She is presently associate professor. She received her doctorate in 1974 from the University of Chicago. Prior to coming to Loyola in 1976, she spent three years at SUNY in Stony Brook, New York. Her major publications have been in the area of poverty and welfare.

Dr. McCourt is an assistant professor at Loyola. She received her Ph.D. degree from the University of Chicago in 1975. She was a study director at the National Opinion Research Center from 1972 to 1976. She is the coauthor with Andrew Greeley and William McCready of *The Catholic School and the Declining Church* and *Working Class Women and Grass Root Politics.*

Dr. McNamara received his Ph.D. degree from Cornell in 1963. He was at Fordham University from 1962 to 1970 and chaired the Department of Sociology there from 1968 to 1970. He was a visiting study director at the National Opinion Research Center in 1966-1967. He has been at Loyola as a professor of sociology since 1970 and was Dean of the College of Arts and Sciences from 1970 to 1973. His major publications have been in the area of the sociology of religion.

The response to this paper was prepared by Dr. Murray L. Gruber, a professor in the School of Social Work of Loyola University. Coming from the University of Michigan, he joined the Loyola faculty this year. His major publications are on management systems in the human services and on inequality in the social services. A number of his articles have appeared in *The Nation.* Since Dr. Gruber is ill, his response will be read by Dean Charles O'Reilly of the School of Social Work.

May I now present Dr. Robert McNamara, who will read the paper jointly conceived by him, Dr. Grønbjerg, and Dr. McCourt, "Race and Distributive Justice in Chicago: Does Loyola Have a Local Responsibility?"

Race and Distributive Justice in Chicago: Does Loyola Have a Local Responsibility?

Dr. Kirsten Grønbjerg
Dr. Kathleen McCourt
Dr. Robert McNamara

Although our primary focus is on race and distributive justice, we are not limiting ourselves to Chicago, but attempt to address the issues on a national basis and in a historical perspective as well. In our conclusion we will argue not only that Loyola has special local responsibilities to address issues of distributive justice, but also that such responsibilities are more clearly understood in a national and historical context.

Black Upward Mobility: Race vs. Class

The biggest obstacle to black upward mobility in the United States is economic class, not race, according to William J. Wilson, a black professor of sociology, who presented his controversial argument in *The Declining Significance of Race* (1978). Although the American Sociological Association bestowed on him one of its annual awards, the Association of Black Sociologists was "outraged over [Wilson's] misrepresentations of the black experience."[1] We are not about to adjudicate this dispute. Rather we shall state two generalizations with which very few would disagree. We shall situate these in Wilson's theory of race relations in the United States; then we shall look at the recent statistical record to see how they stand up; finally we shall show how they connect with the question of institutional responsibilities in general and Loyola's local responsibilities in particular. The first generalization: race is not as effective an obstacle to black upward mobility as it used to be. The second: low economic class is a relatively more formidable obstacle to black upward mobility than it used to be.

Wilson's Theory

If one takes the whole sweep of American history, it is difficult to disagree with Wilson's division of American race relations into three stages of black-white contact. Each period embodies "a different form of racial stratification structured by the particular arrangement of the economy and polity."[2]

In the antebellum period the important locale was the southern plantation. The forces of production—technology—were almost entirely manual labor used to grow and pick cotton, tobacco, and food; the social relations of production were based on the master-slave relationship. Political power was in the hands of the slave owners who used it "to legitimate, reinforce and regulate patterns of racial inequality."[3] Racism was the white man's paternalism, reinforced by his ideology or even by his religion. Blacks were defined as subservient children, unable to grow up.

The second period was characterized by industrial expansion, class conflict, and racial oppression. In the South after the brief Reconstruction period, whites succeeded in reducing blacks to a position of near-slavery once again, both economically and politically. Whites, including the poor whites competing with blacks for jobs, devised the extensive Jim Crow legislation that kept blacks in their inferior economic and political place. The paternalism of the antebellum period gave way to a more naked and visible ideology of segregation based on doctrines of biological and cultural inferiority.

Not only in the South did economic competition cause trouble between the races during the period of industrial expansion. The migration of blacks from South to North, from rural to urban areas, began on a large scale in the 1920s, and from the 1940s to the mid-1960s became an internal human migration unmatched in size in American history. Blacks came for jobs and needed places to live. The whites who stood to lose in the competition for jobs, housing, and local political control fought for what they had. Racism displayed an interpretation of blacks as both inferior and menacing.

The political events leading to the modified race relations of the modern industrial period are recognizable only in hindsight. Certainly the 1954 Supreme Court decision defining separate education as unconstitutional stands as a landmark along with various presidential decisions and executive orders. The civil rights marches, boycotts, and sit-ins of the 1960s; the civil rights legislation of 1964 and 1965; the enforcement of affirmative action programs—all these were political events aimed at a social and legal redefinition of relations between blacks and whites.

56

With respect to the system of production during the modern industrial period, modern technology has *decreased* the proportion of unskilled jobs available to all workers, while it has *increased* the proportion of skilled jobs, especially in the service and government sectors. These jobs have education as their major prerequisite. Inner-city blacks (and Hispanics as well) are more likely to fall short of the educational requirements. Many of them are therefore eligible only for the menial, unskilled jobs that not only lead nowhere, but are also increasingly scarce. Result: an underclass, disproportionately black and Hispanic, that is chronically or sporadically unemployed, and in many cases unemployable and demoralized.

Notice that Wilson calls this group an under*class*. Its members lack the skills to connect with the higher technology jobs that would then be available to them. Many blacks *could* get these jobs in the service sector and in the government. Blacks who have somehow obtained an education have gone on to land such jobs, frequently with assistance from affirmative action programs, and they constitute what Wilson calls the newly emerged black middle class. They have succeeded despite their race because of the middle-class skills they possess. That is the gist of Wilson's argument.

While we find this argument persuasive, a number of considerations must be given some attention before we proceed. (1) We must approach with caution the notion of a black middle class, because we are talking about only a small proportion of the black population. (2) While there is less individual racist behavior in the employment area, racism, including institutionalized racism, has by no means disappeared from education, government, housing, business, or law. (3) The new black middle class may be in trouble in the future as a result of the current recession and the Reagan administration's moves to reduce jobs in the service sector and to retreat from strong support for affirmative action plans.

Blacks in the Context of Minority Groups

Although our particular focus is on Chicago, we need first to examine some of the larger questions about the situation of blacks and other minority groups in the United States in general. Specifically, to what extent has the black experience been similar to that of other minority groups? Experiences of these groups in the United States have been varied, as the result of some readily identifiable factors, including the particular composition and character of the minority population and the historical circumstances under which the group arrived in this country. The nature of minority stereotypes and the basis of the group's separation from American society, whether its members were "left behind," "kept in their place," or partially accepted as "hyphenated Americans," were important in shaping the barriers which have restricted the group's participation in the cultural and economic life of the nation.[4] Such barriers are particularly formidable when they coincide with low socioeconomic status.

Despite differences in experiences, barriers to full participation have been commonly faced by minority groups. At various times in history, most minority groups have faced not only political and social discrimination, but have been relegated to particular niches in the economy. Some of the smaller minority groups are concentrated in niches which depend on an expanding economy and a certain amount of discretionary income. Larger minority groups, notably blacks and Hispanics, are more heavily involved in basic industry and the unskilled service sector, and depend upon long-term economic growth for employment. When growth declines, unemployment goes up first and most dramatically for the minorities. This is what underlies most minority group conflicts, although such conflicts are often enlarged beyond material interests into status politics.

In important respects, however, the historical experience of blacks has been significantly different from that of other minority groups. Blacks occupy a unique position among American minority groups because of the size and visibility of their population. Furthermore, slavery and its accompanying ideologies have made racial stereotypes and prejudices particularly difficult to overcome. Finally, as Wilson indicates, it is only in very recent years that blacks have been able to penetrate into the central political and economic activities of the nation. Ironically, blacks gained access to new job opportunities just when those opportunities were being limited to persons with particular educational achievements. By virtue of their rural, southern background, their continuing subjections to discrimination and inferior education, blacks were unable to participate fully in the recent transformations and expansions of the economy.

Access to good jobs today depends to a considerable extent on one's ability to purchase quality education. Middle-class black parents are able, although often with difficulty, to provide their children with good education and thus help them obtain good jobs. Both level of education and income can still be fairly well predicted from knowledge about minority status. This is witness to the continuing importance of race in structuring the relationship of the individual to central institutions, such as education and occupation.

The evidence for this is perhaps most compelling when we examine data on the incidences of poverty. In any comparison between whites and blacks, blacks are at least twice as likely to be poor as whites (see Table 1). But there are strong indications

Table 1 Incidences of Poverty in Different Categories

| | Percentage Poor | | | | | |
| | Whites | | | Blacks | | |
Population Category	1959	1969	1978	1959	1969	1978
All persons	18.1	9.5	8.7	55.1	32.2	30.6
Unrelated individuals						
Males	33.8	24.1	14.7	46.4	36.5	30.9
Females	50.3	36.6	23.6	67.1	55.5	46.4
Elderly males	–	18.1	8.3	–	46.2	26.7
Elderly females	–	27.2	14.7	–	53.1	39.0
Farm residents	–	17.1	11.2	–	63.9	34.4
Central city residents	13.8	9.7	10.2	40.8	24.3	31.5
Southerners	26.8	12.4	10.2	68.5	40.8	34.1
Family heads						
Males	13.3	6.0	4.7	43.3	17.9	11.8
Females	34.8	25.7	23.5	65.4	56.3	50.6
Children in families						
Male-headed	17.4	6.7	6.8	60.6	25.0	17.6
Female-headed	64.6	45.2	39.9	81.6	68.2	66.4
Families						
Head aged 14-24	22.5	12.8	13.2	–	31.2	49.1
Head aged 25-44	12.8	6.3	7.6	–	26.6	28.7
With 2 children	12.2	6.6	8.1	–	24.7	31.9
With 5+ children	44.6	18.5	26.6	–	53.1	61.5
Head unemployed	28.1	12.9	19.8	–	45.9	43.9
Head employed	10.3	4.2	5.0	–	17.0	13.8
Head worked						
F-T YR	7.6	2.5	2.1	–	11.0	6.3

Source: U.S. Department of Commerce, Bureau of the Census, *Current Population Reports, Series P-60, No. 124.* "Characteristics of the Population Below the Poverty Level: 1978" (Washington, D.C.: Government Printing Office, June 1980), Tables 1-6.
Note: *Head worked F-T YR* means that the head of the family worked full-time for 50-52 weeks during the year in which the income was reported. Also note that data for some groups were not available for 1959.

that the structure of poverty has changed over the last twenty years or so, and that the overall reduction in poverty has affected some blacks more than others. Black males have been catching up: black male heads of households were 2.5 times as likely to be poor as white male heads of households in 1978, compared to 3.2 times as likely in 1959. Black heads of households aged twenty-five to forty-four are now 3.8 times as likely to be poor as their white counterparts, compared to 4.2 times as likely in 1968. Furthermore, for blacks in the labor force, there has been a significant reduction in excess poverty relative to whites between 1979 and 1978.

For black women, blacks who are aged, southerners, or living in families headed by young adults (aged fourteen to twenty-four), however, poverty relative to whites with the same characteristics has *increased* over the last twenty years. For residents of central cities too, while the 1960s showed some improvements, this gain was lost by 1978, when blacks in central cities again were more than three times as likely to be poor as whites in those areas.

Thus the distribution of poverty and economic opportunities has become quite different over the last twenty years. Sex and family status appear to have become a particularly important combination. We have what is referred to as the "feminization" of poverty, with female-headed families consistently poorer than male-headed families. While such families were almost three times as likely to be poor as male-headed families in 1959, today they are six times as likely to be poor. Children in families headed by women are almost seven times as likely to be poor.

As these data suggest, the growth and transformation of the American economy over the last twenty years have not affected all population groups to the same extent, or even in the same way. We look to social structures for explanations. Residents of old, industrial, central cities like Chicago have experienced increased rates of unemployment and poverty, reflecting the loss of jobs and economic wealth to the suburbs and the sunbelt. Males and those able to participate in the labor force benefitted disproportionately from the increase in the overall number of jobs and various job training programs. The absence of child care facilities and family planning programs may be especially critical in keeping women poor.

For those who are able to find employment, Wilson's data,

along with the arguments of Braverman (1974), point to the continuing existence of the secondary labor market, characterized by low wages, unstable and part-time employment. Blacks now share this labor market with Hispanics, especially undocumented Mexican workers. As Wilson points out, however, even the secondary labor market has become better educated. Job competition is thus particularly difficult for those with very low levels of education. But even some high school training is no guarantee of entering the primary labor market, where fringe benefits, employment security, and opportunities for advancement exist. This phenomenon of increased educational requirements for jobs at all levels is known as "credentialism." The technical requirements of many jobs have increased, and more education may actually be needed to perform the jobs. The major growth in occupations has been among those requiring high levels of education or training. But credentialism means that formal educational achievements are being used, sometimes arbitrarily, as a means of screening applicants for positions, while the number of people with advanced training, especially those with undergraduate and graduate degrees, increases faster than the supply of jobs requiring such training. This has also reduced the incidence of internal recruitment, or promotion from within a given company. These trends have certainly benefitted educational institutions like Loyola, and it would be detrimental to our own economic opportunities to suggest a rejection of these tendencies particularly in view of declining college age cohorts in the future. Nevertheless, a careful examination of the implications of these trends for such institutions is in order.

Distributive Justice and Responsibility

We have argued that recent changes in American society have significantly affected economic opportunities. The most important of these changes have been the following: the declining significance of race; the increasing significance of class; the declining job opportunities in central cities; the persistence of constraints on individuals' ability to use available opportunities, and the strengthening link between educational and economic opportunities. The answer to the larger question of what, if anything, should be done about such trends depends on one's understanding of what should be the basis of American society, and what is or should be the nature of citizenship in this society.

A discussion of the rights and obligations of members of this society is integral to a consideration of the proper roles of various institutions in the society. Here, because of time constraints, we shall discuss only citizenship rights, although we would maintain that education is crucial for being able to perform various citizenship duties in an informed and responsible manner.

Citizenship rights are of several varieties. Following the discussion of Marshall (1964) we are suggesting that there are basically three types of citizenship: (1) civil rights, such as the right to free speech, religion, and due process; (2) political rights, such as the right to vote, hold political office, and engage in a certain range of political activities, and (3) social rights, or the right to share in a modicum of the nation's economic and cultural heritage. Marshall argues that these rights are imperfectly extended to members of a given society. In most developed societies, civil rights are the most extended, followed by political rights, and then by social rights.[5] Over time, all forms of citizenship rights have been extended, largely in negotiations between individual citizens and public authorities. Thus the courts have been the central institution in extending civil and political rights, since these are most easily identified by specific infringements on individual liberty. The extension of social rights, on the other hand, has increased only with the growth of government, in which the central responsibility for social rights has increasingly been located, as seen in the development of the welfare state. Of secondary importance, but crucial as well, is the role played by nonpublic institutions, both voluntarily and in response to government regulations, in increasing economic opportunities to formerly excluded sections of American society.

Social rights are the central focus of this paper: access to jobs, to culture, to participation. That social rights are, or should be, available to all would seem to be a central goal of a democratic society. If we assume the validity of this goal, and we do, we are facing the central question of distributive justice and responsibility for achieving such justice.

The activities of, and assumption of responsibilities by, three central institutions appear to be critical. These are: government, the private economy, and educational institutions, especially colleges and universities. We shall discuss only the latter here. Under credentialism, these institutions have become particularly important in shaping the economic opportunities of individuals. The declining economies of the North and the East suggest that institutions of higher education will be particularly significant for the populations of those regions, if they are to be able to compete for the decreasing number of jobs, or prepare themselves for successful migration to the sunbelt. Finally, universities, by virtue of their emphases on the production and the dissemination of new knowledge, bear central responsibility for documenting the imperfect extension of social citizenship. Such knowledge is essential for the designing of policies by all institutions.

In our view the responsibilities of colleges and universities like Loyola extend beyond the production of knowledge about the distribution of justice. As educational institutions they train students for employment, providing them with skills and special knowledge useful in employment. They have become the gatekeeping institutions under credentialism, and the extent to which they operate on the principles of extending social rights will have critical influence on those who have traditionally been denied access to economic opportunities. This justifies affirmative action policies, and we want to reiterate our strong support for such policies. The barriers to economic opportunities have become greater for those who do not make the first cut into college. Affirmative action and vigorous pursuit of extension of educational opportunities are critical just to keep the odds for economic opportunities from deteriorating.

Educational institutions also educate for civic responsibility, creating informed, responsible, and able members of society, who can understand social issues, perceive their own role in civic affairs, and develop the necessary confidence to be actively involved. Closely related to this role of educational institutions is the final responsibility, what we may call transformation for humanist citizenship. This more ideological and possibly more controversial role, namely the development of a broader sense of social responsibility, involves the acceptance of the social rights of peripheral groups in the society, and sensitivity to their needs. At this point a concern with values and ethics becomes central to our consideration. Specifically, are the values of equal social rights those we endorse, and what ethical issues do we face when we attempt to insure such rights?

Loyola's Responsibilities and Distributive Justice

To examine Loyola's specific responsibilities under distributive justice, it is necessary to situate Loyola within the Catholic educational system in Chicago. We shall also examine Loyola's students, their background, and their aspirations, to provide the context for Loyola's responsibility in distributive justice as we see it.

Loyola and Chicago's Educational System

Catholic education in the United States began as a system for educating minorities, initially children of Irish Catholic immigrants, later other European Catholic groups as well. Historically the Catholic schools had two functions: (1) to provide an education and training for children who were not likely to be fully accepted into the existing network of public and private schools; (2) to provide that education in a context that would "protect the faith" and further the religious development of the young. The hierarchy's admonition that for these reasons children should be educated in Catholic schools was taken seriously by parents.[6]

The peak in Catholic education at the primary and secondary levels was reached in the 1950s and 1960s. By 1965 there were over 14,000 schools and 3.5 million students. By 1975 Catholic elementary education nationally was in decline: schools were down 24 percent and enrollments 35 percent.[7] The Chicago Archdiocese school system, covering Cook and Lake counties, has suffered similar declines each year since the peak of 1965. In 1980, however, the Chicago parochial school system saw a modest gain of around 500 students over the previous year. This increase is notable, according to *The Chicago Reporter*'s recent (February 1981) article, "because it is not a result of a white student exodus from Chicago public schools or a boost in enrollment in suburban Catholic schools." Rather, the increase is due to the number of black and Latino children attending Catholic schools in Chicago (see Table 2). Between 1973 and 1980, minorities in Chicago's Catholic school system rose from 31 percent of the total enrollment to 43 percent, and now include 29,000 black children. Many of these are poor; 42 percent of those in predominantly black Catholic schools received some public aid last year, compared to only 2 percent of the students in predominantly white Catholic schools. Also, more than half the black students in Chicago's Catholic schools are not Catholic.

Black parents are sending their children to Catholic schools for reasons different from those that motivated earlier generations of white Catholics. Black children are not unaccepted in public schools and, at least among those who are not Catholic, there is not a concern for protecting and nurturing their religious beliefs. But black parents are looking for a better education for their children and, according to *The Reporter* article, they are looking for discipline, a more accessible school administration, and most importantly, an education that emphasizes values. This transformation has not occurred without problems. Many Catholics, for example, resent having the resources of their church and school system go towards the education of non-Catholics.

Table 2 Enrollment Changes in Chicago Catholic Schools

	Elementary Schools			*High Schools*		
	1973	*1979*	*1980*	*1973*	*1979*	*1980*
White	69,725	43,772	43,225	30,514	24,189	23,634
Minority	34,457	37,840	39,743	9,947	10,603	10,548
Black	22,328	22,469	23,107	—*	5,888	5,688
Latino	10,726	12,723	13,765	—*	4,175	4,144
Other	1,403	2,648	2,871	—*	540	716
Totals	104,182	81,612	82,968	40,461	34,792	34,182

Source: Office for Catholic Education, Archdiocese of Chicago; analyzed by *The Chicago Reporter*.
*Not available.

Our impression is that there are two relationships operating between black students and Catholic schools. (1) Some blacks are Catholic; in the Chicago Archdiocese, the figure is around 90,000. As a religious group, these Catholic blacks have been more upwardly mobile than non-Catholic blacks precisely because they have been able to take advantage of the Catholic school system. (2) Most blacks are not Catholic, but many wish to take advantage of Catholic schools (elementary through college) nonetheless, because these are seen as more effective in providing children with a sound education in a more personalized and value-oriented environment. Neither of these statements can be proved or disproved with the data at hand, but both have a social reality in the minds of those affected by them.

If these statements are true—and there are indications and preliminary research to suggest that they are—then Catholic schools in this country and this city may take at least some of the credit for helping to shape the black middle class of which Wilson speaks. We believe something comparable to the transformation of the Catholic school system at the lower levels has occurred at the college level. Catholic colleges too are seeing a shift in the population they serve and consequently are finding it necessary to reformulate their mission.

Loyola's Students: Background and Aspiration

Loyola is a Jesuit university, as well as a private and midwestern one. But this statement tells us little. The differences among Jesuit universities seem to be at least as significant as their similarities, and the background of Loyola's undergraduate students is distinctive. Table 3 (pages 68-69) shows that entering freshmen in 1980 (and in 1972) came from Chicago area families whose socioeconomic status was considerably lower than the national average for either public or private universities. Their status, however, is similar to that of students attending other Midwest institutions of higher education, including public and private two-year and four-year colleges. But the ambitions of Loyola students and their families are as high as those of students attending private universities with tougher admissions criteria and much higher average levels of socioeconomic status. With respect to the professional fields of dentistry, medicine, law, and nursing, Loyola's students are extraordinarily ambitious, much more so than all students in private universities, and they have been so since at least 1972. Loyola's freshmen want very much to get ahead, way ahead, of their parents; that is what they seem to mean when a disproportionately high number of freshmen (78 percent) state that its good academic reputation was a very important reason for their choosing Loyola.

We can infer two other reasons for attending Loyola: financial and religious. The combination of Illinois state grants, Loyola's lower tuition, and less stringent admissions standards compared to other private institutions apparently attracts ambitious students who, for all sorts of reasons—mostly financial, we think— do not want to travel far to go to college. The religious factor is still important in attracting students, although it may be declining in importance. In 1972, 83 percent of Loyola's freshmen came from Catholic homes, and 64 percent from Catholic high schools; in 1980, only 75 percent came from Catholic homes and only half came from Catholic high schools. Unfortunately, we simply do not know what role Loyola's reputation as a Catholic institution plays in attracting non-Catholic students. But it is clear that the Catholic religious vision that was once pervasive at Loyola is no longer shared by many students and faculty members. It has become optional and "privatized"; nonbelief is no longer surprising on our campus.

Because of changes in the parochial school system, an increasing proportion of the population from which Loyola has traditionally drawn its students will belong to racial and ethnic groups that have not attended Loyola in great numbers in the past. Already minority students at Loyola have almost doubled in the past decade, from 12 percent of the incoming freshmen in 1972 to 20 percent in 1980. The proportion of blacks increased slightly (8.9 percent to 9.4 percent); the proportion of Hispanics (Mexican-Americans and Puerto Ricans) increased from 2 percent to 5.5 percent; the proportion of Orientals from 1 percent to 3.8 percent. We can expect the number of minority and non-Catholic students to continue to grow at Loyola.

Upward mobility may be many a young person's *motive* for coming to Loyola—it always was—but the *consequence* of four years at Loyola should be much more than that. This involves another vision based on distributive justice and closely connected with Loyola's traditional concern for the humanities, especially for philosophy and theology. Distributive justice is not upward mobility. Its technical definition is essentially the proportionate sharing of the common good by all. But its application to our society demands that an educational institution in Loyola's position strive to bring a fuller share of participation to its students in the economy and in the civic and social life of the area. We can bring this fuller share to groups whose race or economic class has kept their share small in the past, just as in the past we brought a fuller share to groups whose ethnic backgrounds or religion kept their shares small.

Loyola's role here is not just to provide the full rewards of citizenship, i.e., status and income, to minority groups. But greater participation in civil and social life brings greater responsibility in its turn. If we can inculcate this responsibility among

Table 3 The American Freshman: Selected National Norms

Norms	1980					1972				
	Loyola	Midwest	Priv.U. SimAdm	All Priv.U.	All Pub.U.	Loyola	Midwest	All Univ.	All Priv.U.	All Pub.U.
Race										
White	80.2	92.3	86.2	88.3	91.3	87.6	92.9	94.7	92.5	91.9
Black	9.4	5.4	7.0	5.5	6.5	8.9	5.6	3.5	4.8	5.8
Hispanic	5.5	1.0	2.8	2.2	0.8	2.0	0.6	0.7	1.3	0.6
High School Rank										
Top group	56.2	47.7	53.2	69.0	54.3	61.6	50.1	6.5	70.7	64.1
2d group	26.0	23.8	24.7	17.1	23.6	29.7	32.5	26.3	21.1	27.8
Av. H.S. Grade										
A or A+	12.9	10.8	14.1	26.6	13.3	6.6	7.2	12.2	21.2	9.7
A–	12.5	15.6	16.2	21.7	16.3	14.3	12.1	16.7	20.6	15.6
B+	26.6	20.7	24.7	21.6	22.3	26.1	20.0	24.3	23.2	24.6
Roman Catholic										
Self	74.6	34.6	52.6	41.8	31.1	72.2	31.5	26.8	27.9	23.7
Parents	75.6	35.5	54.7	43.4	32.0	83.2	36.1	32.5	44.1	29.3
Public H.S.	49.3	84.2	65.2	68.8	86.1	31.9	81.8	84.0	67.5	88.6
Parents' Income										
Under $20,000	35.3	34.3	28.0	14.1	18.2	78.5	75.1	67.5	56.9	70.5
Over $40,000	19.7	19.5	30.5	37.7	22.9	4.7	4.2	7.1	14.1	5.2
Father's Occupation										
Blue Collar	27.0	20.1	14.1	10.3	14.8	33.8	23.5	16.3	14.1	17.0
Doctor, Dentist	5.5	2.6	5.5	7.6	2.8	4.6	2.3	3.5	6.6	2.7
Lawyer	1.7	1.7	3.4	4.5	2.1	1.8	1.3	2.2	3.8	1.8
Businessman	28.9	30.4	39.0	38.0	34.3	29.4	30.8	35.3	43.8	40.8

Father's Education										
H.S. Unfinished	23.0	14.2	11.6	8.0	10.9	23.6	20.9	13.3	11.5	13.8
College Degree	15.4	19.6	23.7	24.8	20.2	14.8	16.3	23.0	23.8	22.8
Graduate Degree	14.9	15.1	22.7	31.5	7.0	10.6	10.6	16.9	23.4	15.1
Professional Aspiration										
Lawyer	13.9	4.4	9.5	10.2	5.3	10.7	5.0	7.0	10.8	5.9
Doctor	26.9	4.1	8.3	12.7	4.6	29.1	6.5	9.7	16.8	7.7
Dentist	6.0	1.1	3.1	2.1	1.3	—	—	—	—	—
Nurse	10.6	3.9	3.6	2.2	3.3	6.9	4.4	3.4	3.3	3.4
Totals	57.4	13.5	24.5	27.2	14.5	46.7	15.9	20.1	29.9	17.0
Biological Sciences as Major Area	16.6	3.6	6.0	7.5	4.5	8.9	3.4	5.4	5.7	5.3
Home to College over 50 Miles	10.4	60.0	57.6	72.4	68.5	9.8	55.4	70.5	68.2	71.2
Planned Highest Degree										
Master's	25.7	30.2	33.6	33.1	33.0	21.6	26.1	27.7	28.5	27.5
Doctorate	12.9	7.7	11.9	15.4	9.3	11.7	7.8	11.5	16.3	10.1
M.D.	23.8	7.6	11.5	16.7	9.0	28.7	8.4	12.3	18.1	10.7
LL.D.	9.9	4.6	10.0	11.2	5.4	8.4	4.8	6.7	10.6	5.6
Totals	72.3	50.1	67.0	76.4	56.7	70.4	47.1	58.2	73.5	53.4
Financing College "Major Concern"	22.9	17.0	16.5	14.4	14.4	19.3	15.9	14.1	13.4	14.3
No Parental Aid	28.8	27.5	20.5	15.5	21.1	—	—	—	—	—
BEOG	28.3	30.0	28.4	24.3	23.3	—	—	—	—	—
State Scholarship	46.8	18.9	24.1	22.1	13.6	—	—	—	—	—
College Grant	14.5	18.0	24.7	29.1	9.2	—	—	—	—	—

Note: These data were taken from the American Council on Education's 1972 and 1980 reports as well as from ACE's private report to Loyola.

all our students, as we almost automatically provide upward mobility, we shall be doing our traditional job, but in a new and challenging way.

In our judgment Loyola has a definite local responsibility to disadvantaged groups, because of both its history and its capabilities. We suggest that the articulation of this responsibility, plus its reflection in the activity of our admissions officers and of our faculty in the construction of appropriate courses and curricula, would sharpen the focus of our common vision at Loyola.

We have not spoken about research, but research plays a role in our scheme of things, especially for faculty in the social sciences. The black underclass will not be counted among the freshmen at Loyola or any other college. But a further understanding of the social dynamics that create and sustain such inequities, as well as possible routes to a solution, can be explored through research. Here too the Loyola community has a role to play in seeking social justice.

Catholic schools at all levels have taken on the role of educating black students, elementary and secondary schools much more so than universities. The more problematic issue arises around the question of the atmosphere within which this is being done. At Loyola we must ask ourselves: are we educating black students because "that's where the bodies are" in Chicago and we need all the students we can get these days? Or because we must have a certain percentage of minority students in order to "look good on paper" to federal agencies that might be sources of funds? Are we genuinely comfortable with an argument that our university, like Catholic elementary and secondary schools, has changed, and that as we move toward the end of the twentieth century we will be training a new leadership for Chicago and for America? While we still continue to educate white, Catholic students will we be—can we be—equally committed to the nonwhite, non-Catholic students? If so, much more can and must be done to achieve distributive justice.

Notes

1. Charles Vert Willie, ed., *The Caste and Class Controversy,* as quoted by Omi in his review of W. J. Wilson's *The Declining Significance of Race: Blacks and Changing American Institutions,* p. 119.

2. *The Declining Significance of Race: Blacks and Changing American Institutions* (Chicago: University of Chicago Press, 1978), p. 12.

3. Ibid., p. 17.

4. See Grønbjerg, Street, and Suttles, chapters 6 and 7, especially pp. 95-96, for a fuller discussion of these issues.

5. Perhaps one of the ideological differences we experience with established Communist nations concerns the possible reversal of this order of rights in terms of importance and degree of extension.

6. Indeed, until about twenty-five years ago, in some circles it was defined as sinful for Catholic parents not to send their children to Catholic schools, if they could afford to do so.

7. Interestingly, enrollment in Catholic colleges increased by almost 40,000 between 1965 and 1975, reflecting the impact of the baby boom on higher educational institutions.

Bibliography

American Council on Education. *The American Freshman: National Norms for Fall, 1972.* Washington, D.C., American Council on Education Research Reports, Vol. 7, No. 5, 1973.

Astin, Alexander W., et al. *The American Freshman: National Norms for Fall, 1980.* The Cooperative Institutional Research Program, American Council on Education, Graduate School of Education, University of California at Los Angeles, 1981.

Braverman, Harry. *Labor and Monopoly Capital.* New York: Monthly Review Press, 1974.

Grønbjerg, Kirsten; Street, David; and Suttles, Gerald. *Poverty and Social Change.* Chicago: University of Chicago Press, 1978.

Marshall, T. H. *Class Citizenship and Social Development.* Chicago: University of Chicago Press, 1964.

Omi, Michael. Review of William J. Wilson's *The Declining Significance of Race: Blacks and Changing American Institutions* in *The Insurgent Sociologist,* Vol. 10, No. 2 (Fall 1980), pp. 118-122.

U.S., Bureau of the Census, *Current Population Reports,* Series B-60, No. 124. "Characteristics of the Population Below the Poverty Level: 1978." Washington, D.C.: Government Printing Office, 1980.

Willie, Charles Vert, ed., *The Caste and Class Controversy.* Bayside, N.Y.: General Hall, Inc., 1979.

Wilson, William J. *The Declining Significance of Race: Blacks and Changing American Institutions.* Chicago: University of Chicago Press, 1978.

A Response to "Race and Distributive Justice in Chicago"
Dr. Murray Gruber

It is indicative of the complexities of the subject of race and justice that so much has been written, what is written usually provokes controversy, and social change comes but slowly. The paper by Professors Grønbjerg, McCourt, and McNamara lands squarely in the complexities of race and justice; it will no doubt provoke debate; and it may provide impetus for coming to grips with difficult questions of institutional change. It is in my judgment a splendid example of the coupling of the analytic and the normative, the *is* and the *ought*.

There are three issues in this paper to which I would like to attend: (1) the issue of race vs. class; (2) the linkage between education and occupational mobility; (3) Loyola's role vis à vis the issue of race and distributive justice.

Black Upward Mobility: Race vs. Class
To summarize briefly, the authors have suggested that skills and education (as well as a variety of political and legal factors) have enabled an upwardly mobile black middle class to gain access to good jobs. For this black middle class *race is not so formidable a barrier to upward mobility* as it used to be. On the other hand, there is an impacted, stagnant underclass who fall short of the educational and skill requirements of an increasingly demanding occupational structure, and therefore they are either unemployable or locked into mostly low-wage, dead-end jobs. For them *low socioeconomic class* is a relatively more formidable block than it used to be.

Wisely, I believe, the authors have suggested several cautions. First, that the size of the black middle class is relatively small. Additionally, the gains of this class are precarious and are placed in jeopardy by the policies of the Reagan administration. Indeed these policies may render moot our academic discussions of race vs. class. While I underscore the authors' cautions, I am inclined to be even more cautious (and perhaps more pessimistic) than they. I suggest for example that even the *modest* size of the black middle class is overestimated, and some gains have *already* eroded. Specifically I refer to the fact that between 1969 and 1972 the proportion of middle- and upper-income families increased from 21 to 25 percent, topped out at 25 percent, and by 1975 had declined to 23 percent.

The second issue here pertains to the questions, who are the black middle class, by what criteria are they middle class, and do these criteria give an accurate picture? Occupational attainment is but one measure of class, a measure that tends to inflate the size of the black middle class. Income gives a rather different picture. Median income for black males in middle-class occupations in 1975 was as follows: black managers, $12,000; black professionals, $10,700, black craftsmen, $9,000; black salesmen, $7,000. What seems to be middle class in terms of occupational categories is not middle class in terms of income. Neither $7,000, $9,000, nor even $10,000 was adequate in 1975 to buy into the middle class according to the standards of the Bureau of Labor Statistics. Parenthetically I note here that for each of the aforementioned occupations, black earnings were lower than white earnings.

Education and Mobility

I come now to a second major question, "What determines income?" It is an article of deep belief that education is the instrument of all forms of progress. A subset of this doctrine is the argument that education is positively related to economic success, and that a relatively more equal distribution of education would therefore lead to a more equal distribution of income. Indeed human capital economists have argued persuasively that education is an investment that increases people's productivity; it increases their contribution to the economic system, and consequently increases the economic rewards they receive. Cross-sectional analysis, that is, analysis between groups, supports this argument. Yet time series data show no evidence that economic equality accompanies increased educational quality. As the economist Lester Thurow has pointed out, we might be more questioning about the productivity impact of education and its equalizing effects. To be sure, the occupational hierarchy is greatly segregated by education; the more education, the better one's chances for good jobs. But it may well be that in a labor market with *chronically high unemployment* the function of education is less to confer skills and increase productivity and higher wages, and more to certify the worker's "trainability." In other words, given a lineup of workers for particular jobs, education is used as a screening device. The relevant question is, how defensible is this practice? If, as some studies suggest, informal on-the-job training is the way that most workers learn their jobs, then perhaps we need to modify our assumption that the poor are poor because they have gotten bad education. Indeed a full employment economy with guaranteed jobs, and a much greater equalization of labor market wages, are probably more likely to be effective for the poor than reliance on education.

Loyola and Distributive Justice

Still, for the foreseeable future, it seems clear that our educational institutions will bear the burden of facilitating the upward mobility of blacks and other minorities. Leaving aside all the other benefits of education, in this limited context of economic mobility, education is indeed a defensible necessity, notwithstanding the relative effectiveness of other possible measures.

What role then does Loyola have in this question of mobility and justice? Professors Grønbjerg, McCourt, and McNamara have presented a challenging argument. They have discussed the demographic shifts in Catholic education, and they have pointed out that Catholic education began as a system for educating minorities. With considerable eloquence they have urged a new commitment—the interests of justice call us to serve blacks and other minorities.

While the authors' analysis has emphasized changing demographics and changing responsibilities, I should like to look at this from a somewhat different angle of vision, emphasizing the emergence of what has been called "third sector" organizations. By third sector I mean organizations that were entirely private in character, sectarian and nonsectarian alike, and could therefore pursue their own self-defined purposes. Increasingly, however, there is a growing "publicness" of such institutions and along with it, changes in the goal structure of these institutions. Leaving aside formal charters, these changes, as in the case of Loyola, have been brought about by changes in the financial base. Consider for example that 20 percent of our revenues

74

come from government grants. Or we can look at the matter in terms of public revenues as a proportion of tuition and fees. Exclusive of the Guaranteed Student Loan Program, of about eight million dollars in fiscal year 1979-80, Loyola received 3.7 million federal dollars and 14.4 million state dollars through National Direct Student Loans, Basic Education Opportunity Grants, Supplementary Educational Opportunity Grants, College Work-Study, and Illinois State Program. All told, of Loyola's tuition and fee income, federal and state funds comprised 24.8 percent. Let us set this side by side with the black population at Loyola, 1980-81: 10.8 percent at the undergraduate level and 3.5 percent in the graduate and professional schools.

Were not the growing "publicness" of institutions like Loyola a fact of life, the problems of race and justice would still be with us. In light of the changing character of private institutions there may be an even more pressing necessity to confront changing institutional purposes. In any event I can do no better than to leave you with the last question posed by my colleagues: "While we still continue to educate white Catholic students will we be—can we be—equally committed to the nonwhite, non-Catholic students?" For us at Loyola, changing demographics, questions of justice, and the changing character of social organizations in American society all here converge.

MINISESSION A

Ms. Mary Ellen Druyan: The two speakers in this session are Father Joseph Small and Dr. Ralph Rossum. Father Small has been teaching political science at Loyola since 1954. He has published in the field of local politics and on the ethics of politics. He has been chairman of the Department of Political Science. He is joined today by a newcomer to Loyola, Dr. Ralph Rossum, who is associate professor of political science. Dr. Rossum has previously taught at Memphis State University and Grinnell College. He is the coauthor of six books and has written many articles. It is my pleasure to turn the meeting over to Father Small and Dr. Rossum.

ABSCAM: Testing Ethical Standards
of Public Officials
Father Joseph Small, S.J.

Thank you. This will not be nearly as profound as the paper presented by the sociologists, because we are a more superficial field. But we will try to be a little bit entertaining. The rationale for this presentation is the fact that as we read the papers every day we are informed that public officials are using their offices in ways that we call politically corrupt. What we would like to achieve in an hour is some awareness of the trend or the momentum that is abroad in public life today to curb corruption among public officials.

Looking at the phenomenon of political corruption is something like the famous description of an elephant. We can get contradictory data depending on what we care to focus on. My hope is that in a presentation of this kind we can come to a more balanced view of what the problem is and where we are going as a people. On the one hand, it is easy enough to conclude that public life is private, primitive thievery and that political officials are in it for what they can get. Paul Powell kept his loot in a shoe box. Chicago policemen were caught taking TVs out of retail stores and using squad cars for transport. Bribery and extortion for easement and zoning changes are part of the urban scene. We have had the "Mirage" investigations locally, we have had ABSCAM nationally. All of this persuades us that thievery is going on. However, it is equally easy to document the continual efforts to improve the scene that are not headline-making though they are quite profound in the history of American civilization.

The thesis of this presentation is that slowly but steadily we are raising the temperature of public awareness regarding the responsibilities of political officials. This trend or movement is by no means a simple matter of writing or presenting eloquent rhetoric. These are complex issues. Each problem that we face has the elements of tradition, of complex and conflicting civil rights, and of different sides of a controversy. As an example of the complexity of ethics in public life, the federal government has gone to great lengths to provide us with an example which has come to be called ABSCAM.

I thought with Dr. Rossum that we could look at the complexity of ABSCAM in the light of the movement towards a more public perception of the demands of ethical standards. After I wrote my abstract for this program and it was accepted, I went to the law school and looked for a bibliography on entrapment. Dr. Rossum's name appeared; it turned out that he was an expert on entrapment. So I did not have to bone up on entrapment. I just asked Dr. Rossum to make a presentation.

ABSCAM: On the Nature of Separation
of Powers and Entrapment
Dr. Ralph Rossum

Central to the issue of ethical conduct of public officials are political corruption and its eradication. For political corruption to be eradicated, it must first be detected. This however is no easy task, for, as with other victimless crimes, it is hidden. Once it is detected, those responsible for it must be successfully prosecuted, convicted, and punished. ABSCAM represents an effort along these lines. It is an ingenious, well-planned, and well-executed operation designed by the FBI to root out political corruption at its highest reaches. When the videotape evidence gathered during the ABSCAM operation was introduced at trial and subsequently broadcast on network television, the whole nation was subjected to the disgraceful spectacle of influential members of the Congress boasting of their corrupt influence on Capitol Hill. (It should be mentioned in passing that many Arabs were grievously offended by ABSCAM—which, after all, is an acronym for Arab Scam. While it is understandable that they should have felt libeled, it is not altogether clear whether they took more offense at being presented as givers of bribes or as friends of congressmen.)

ABSCAM has been defended as the only way to deal with this type of political corruption. However, it has also raised in the minds of many two major questions concerning efforts of this kind to seek out, expose, and curb political corruption. Is such an operation consistent with our constitutional commitment to separation of powers? We have in ABSCAM, after all, the executive branch inducing members of the legislative branch into the commission of criminal acts and prosecuting them for these crimes in the judicial branch. Does such an operation amount to entrapment, entrapment being defined as the conception and planning of an offense by the police and the procurement of its commission by one who would not have perpetrated it except for the inducement of the officer?[1] I will argue that the first question concerning separation of powers poses no problem at all and that the second question concerning entrapment ought not to pose one either.

Separation of Powers

ABSCAM is understood by some to violate the principle of separation of powers in that one branch entices the members of another branch to engage in criminal activity. This, they charge, does not indicate the proper regard and respect that one branch owes to another. In the American constitutional system, however, the term "separation of powers" is a misnomer. The national government is not one of strictly separated powers. It consists rather of three coordinate and coequal branches, each performing a blend of functions and thereby balancing, not separating, powers.[2] Richard Neustadt has succinctly described this arrangement as "separated institutions sharing powers."[3] The framers created this arrangement so that each branch could, in the words of *The Federalist,* serve as a "check on the others." By checking, restraining, and limiting each other, the three branches would keep themselves within the "assigned limits of their authority." Separation of power was thus one of several institutional contrivances designed to serve as a "sentinel over the public good."[4]

Such an understanding of separation of powers does not preclude ABSCAM-type operations designed to ferret out political corruption. To the extent that the independence of the legislative branch and the inviolability of the legislative process need special protection from an overreaching executive branch, that protection is to be found in Article I, Section 6. That clause declares that "for any speech or debate in either house," members of the Congress "shall not be questioned in any other place." The speech-and-debate clause, however, is obviously not relevant to ABSCAM. As Chief Justice Burger has noted in *United States* v. *Brewster,* "Taking a bribe is no part of the legislative process or function; it is not a legislative act. It is not, by any conceivable interpretation, an act performed as a part of or even incidental to the role of a legislator."[5]

Entrapment

While ABSCAM has been understood by some to raise questions concerning separation of powers, it has been understood by many more to raise questions concerning entrapment. The concept of entrapment has galvanized the attention of the public at the same time that the technical and legal complexities of the entrapment defense have mystified it. In the section that follows, I will outline the major features of the entrapment defense and indicate why it should pose no particular problem for ABSCAM-type operations.[6]

Entrapment is a widely recognized defense in the criminal law. It is recognized in the federal courts and in forty-nine of the fifty states as well.[7] In the words of Chief Justice Hughes, it is designed to protect persons from prosecution and conviction who, while "otherwise innocent," have been lured by law enforcement officials into the commission of the offense. While this goal is laudable, the entrapment defense limits or restrains political responsibility. The individual is spared the consequences of his ventures into antisocial activity, and he is acquitted, not because he has done anything right to exonerate himself, but because someone else—the governmental official—has done something wrong. In Justice Cardozo's famous complaint: "The criminal is to go free because the constable blundered."[8] For that reason the British courts even today and the American courts until the last quarter of the nineteenth century steadfastly refused to recognize any entrapment defense. As a New York court noted: "We are asked to protect the defendant, not because he is innocent, but because a zealous public officer exceeded his power and held out a bait. The courts do not look to see who held out the bait, but to see who took it."[9] In a democratic republic an individual should be responsible for his actions, regardless of the tempter. Such was the case when Eve, under indictment for consuming fruit from the tree of good and evil, offered unsuccessfully in her defense: "The serpent beguiled me and I did eat." Recognition of the entrapment defense, however, dilutes this sense of responsibility.

Those who have framed the entrapment defense are not unaware of its corrosive effects on political responsibility. Indeed they have sought to limit it in two ways. First, they have denied the entrapment defense to defendants charged with crimes causing or threatening bodily injury.[10] Second, they have refused the defense to those persons who have been led astray by private tempters. If they were to provide for the acquittal of defendants who had been entrapped by private persons, they would encourage collusion and increase the likelihood of contrived defenses. This in turn would make it more difficult to ascertain the truth and perhaps impossible to assign responsibility.

Despite these two exceptions the entrapment defense nevertheless contributes to the undermining of political responsibility, and the question for those who shape and study this defense is to what extent additional limitations on responsibility are to be tolerated. Judges and scholarly commentators alike have tended to divide into two opposing camps. One camp embraces the federal approach, which seeks to keep the issue of the responsibility of the criminal defendant as central as possible. The other supports the "hypothetical person" approach, which in its efforts to protect the government from the "illegal conduct of its officers" and to "preserve the purity of its courts," inadvertently contributes to the further erosion of political responsibility.[11]

The federal approach, so called because it has been adopted by a majority of the Supreme Court justices in each of the major entrapment decisions and is generally followed by the lower federal courts, keeps responsibility central by focusing on the defendant's predisposition to commit the crime for which he is charged.[12] If he was not predisposed to commit crimes of the nature charged, he might avail himself of the defense. However, if he was ready and willing to commit such an offense at any favorable opportunity, then the entrapment defense would fail, regardless of the nature and extent of the government's participation. Because of the focus on the defendant's predisposition, this approach is frequently referred to as the "subjective" test.

The other version of the entrapment defense has been labeled the "hypothetical-person" approach. Expressed in the concurring and dissenting opinions of the same Supreme Court cases that employ the federal approach and in the judicial opinions of several state supreme courts, it concentrates on the quality of police or government conduct. It subscribes to the view that government conduct that falls below certain minimum standards will not be tolerated, thus relieving from criminal responsibility a defendant who commits a crime as a result of such conduct.

This approach will not condone conduct by law enforcement officials that presents too great a risk that a hypothetical, law-abiding person would be induced to commit a crime he would not otherwise have committed. Thus the victim of such conduct, although technically guilty, will be relieved of criminal responsibility, and further prosecution will be barred. Proponents of this approach hope to deter unlawful governmental activity in the instigation of crime and to preserve the purity of the criminal justice system. As with all questions involving the legality of law enforcement methods, the hypothetical-person approach submits the issue of entrapment to the judge, while the jury generally decides the issue under the federal defense. Because of its exclusive concentration on the conduct of the police, this approach is often referred to as the "objective" test.

If ABSCAM is considered in the light of the hypothetical-person test, ABSCAM may well be ruled to be impermissible. It will all depend upon whether the trial court judge finds the FBI's conduct to "fall below standards, to which common feelings respond, for the proper use of governmental power."[13] However, if ABSCAM is considered in the light of the federal defense, ABSCAM will in all probability be sustained. Since the federal defense requires a case-by-case determination of the predisposition of each ABSCAM defendant, the entrapment defense will in all likelihood be the version of the entrapment defense that the federal courts will recognize, as they recognized it in the past. Not only are ABSCAM-type operations necessary to help expose and eliminate political corruption, but the federal defense is far less destructive of the notion of political responsibility than the hypothetical-person defense.

The hypothetical-person defense restricts the political responsibility of the "wary criminal" by providing for his acquittal if he should be offered an inducement that might have tempted a hypothetical, law-abiding person. According to this test, the underlying reason for the entrapment defense is to control the conduct of the police and their agents. Moreover, what is permissible police conduct does not vary according to the particular defendant concerned. The fundamental principle of equality under law requires that police conduct toward all individuals—the wary criminal and the unwary innocent alike—be evaluated in light of the same standard: namely, have they acted in such a manner as is likely to induce to the commission of crime only those persons who are ready and willing to commit further crimes and not others who would normally resist temptation and avoid crime? This standard shifts attention from the character and propensities of the particular defendant to the conduct of the police and the likelihood that it would entrap only those ready and willing to commit crime. It ignores what Justice Holmes so appropriately pointed out in *Schenck* v. *United States*: "The character of every act depends upon the circumstances in which it is done."[14] This is an egregious oversight, for sometimes no fair assessment of the decency of an agent's conduct can be made without considering what the agent knew about the defendant's propensity for crime.

Not only does the hypothetical-person defense restrict the political responsibility of the wary criminal by acquitting him if he should be offered an inducement that would have tempted a hypothetical, law-abiding citizen; it also expands the political accountability of the unwary innocent. It creates a rather substantial risk of convicting nondisposed but ductile defendants. It focuses simply on the nature of the inducements offered by the agent, seeking to ascertain whether he has made an unduly persuasive appeal to friendship, sympathy, or fear; engaged in multiple requests, or suggested the possibility for inordinate gain. If in the estimation of the court the inducements offered would not have tempted a hypothetical, law-abiding person, the fact that the defendant in question succumbed to the temptation will not save him, even if he has never before committed any offense of the nature induced by the agent. Thus the hypothetical-person defense undermines the entire notion of citizen responsibility by, as it were, acquitting wolves and convicting lambs.

A question may well be raised concerning how the police are to be kept from abusing their power if the federal version of the entrapment defense remains in force and continues to focus almost exclusively on the predisposition of the defendant. I would argue with Justice Rehnquist that the notion of political responsibility, so central to the federal defense, provides the answer. An individual is morally and legally obliged to obey the law and is responsible or accountable for all crimes which he may have been predisposed to commit. "Where the predisposition of the defendant to commit the crime" is established, no defense of entrapment is available, despite "governmental misconduct." According to Rehnquist, everyone is responsible for his actions, including the police. He concludes his opinion in *Hampton* v. *United States*: "If the police engage in illegal activity in concert with the defendant beyond the scope of their duties, the remedy lies, not in freeing the equally culpable defendant, but in prosecuting the police under the applicable provisions of state and federal law."[15]

Conclusion

ABSCAM is a valid, permissible, and perhaps even necessary means of seeking out, exposing, and curbing political corruption. It will serve to raise the temperature of awareness of public officials a degree or two. More importantly, it will also raise the temperature of awareness of thoughtful citizens concerning both the American constitutional system of separation of powers and the importance and centrality of individual citizen responsibility in a democratic republic.

Notes

1. See *Sorrels* v. *United States,* 287 U.S. 435, 454 (1932) (Roberts, J., concurring).

2. See Ralph A. Rossum and Gary L. McDowell, *The American Founding: Politics, Statesmanship, and the Constitution* (Port Washington, N.Y.: Kennikat Press, 1981), p. 8.

3. Richard Neustadt, *Presidential Power: The Politics of Leadership* (New York: Science Editions, Inc., 1962), p. 33.

4. See *The Federalist,* Nos. 10, 51.

5. 408 U.S. 501 (1972).

6. One qualification is necessary: I am not arguing that no ABSCAM defendant will be able to raise the entrapment defense successfully. Since the successful raising of the entrapment defense that I advocate (i.e., the federal version, to be discussed below) fundamentally depends upon a showing by the criminal defendant of a lack of predisposition to commit a crime of the nature charged, it may well be the case that particular defendants will be able to convince a court that they were entrapped. I am arguing, however, that under the entrapment defense I support, ABSCAM-type operations are not impermissible, *per se.*

7. Only Tennessee does not recognize any version of the entrapment defense. See *Roden* v. *State,* 209 Tenn. 202, 295, 352 S.W. 2d 227, 228 (1961).

8. *People* v. *Deforc,* 242 N.Y. 13, 21, 150 N.E. 585, 587 (1926).

9. *People* v. *Mills*, 178 N.Y. 274, 289; 70 N.E. 786, 791 (1904).

10. See, for example, Model Penal Code, §2.13 (3) (Official Draft, 1962).

11. The language is from *Casey* v. *United States*, 276 U.S. 413, 425 (1925) (Brandeis, J., dissenting).

12. The major decisions include: *Hampton* v. *United States*, 425 U.S. 484 (1976); *United States* v. *Russell*, 411 U.S. 423 (1973); *Sherman* v. *United States*, 356 U.S. 369 (1958); and *Sorells* v. *United States*, 287 U.S. 435 (1932). For a full discussion of these cases, see Ralph A. Rossum, "The Entrapment Defense and the Supreme Court: On Defining the Limits of Political Responsibility," *Memphis State University Law Review* 7 (Spring, 1977): 367-401.

13. *United States* v. *Russell*, 411 U.S. 423, 441 (1973) (Stewart, J., dissenting).

14. 249 U.S. 47, 52 (1919).

15. 425 U.S. 484, 489-490 (1976).

Father Small's Paper Continued

Let us return to the analogy of the description of the elephant. Where are we as a people? What is happening in our civilization that would help us understand the American mentality toward public service?

From the standpoint of public service, American civilization is a unique phenomenon. Poor, uneducated people came to this completely undeveloped land. Speaking many tongues, they came to an environment where the government offered no help, and they needed everything. They had to make their clothes, homes, and furniture; they had to grow their food. They had grown up in Old World traditions that were frankly elitist. They had no help and they expected no help.

In the Jacksonian era of the 1830s, public servants in the flood tide of immigration saw the advantage of universal white male suffrage; they needed the votes of the people getting off the boats, for all officers had to be elected and elected annually. Such a practice put public officials on a tight leash held by the voters. At the same time the tradition began in which public officials were central, standing between the voting population and the suppliers of services and benefits for this civilization. In the nineteenth century, when urban areas grew quickly, the suppliers were in a position to make unlimited fortunes. To get government contracts they had to have the favor of the local public officials. The local public officials, to stay in office, needed the vote. If they could control the voters, they would be in a position to grant the contracts to the suppliers without having to account for their procedures. To get contracts, suppliers indulged in kickbacks, money under the table. To get votes, public officials wrought favors for the disadvantaged: fruit baskets, coal, jobs, easements of all kinds. Patronage was pervasive.

Where did the money come from for these favors? From the suppliers. A local official who later went to jail addressed one of my classes some years ago. A student asked: "Alderman, there is talk that some aldermen take 5 percent back from their ward patronage. What do you think about that?" He answered, "I think it's all right since our party needs financial support; there are, however, better ways to make money." And he went to jail. What was happening in Chicago is that aldermen were pouring out large sums of money to the poor. They weren't getting the money from the poor; they were getting it from the suppliers. Although there were some efforts at reform, these practices continued until after World War II.

My theory is that the post-World-War-II era is a kind of watershed in the field of political ethics. Take accountability. We see in the newspapers how much so-and-so gave to Jane Byrne's fund raising. This is new. We hadn't a clue about how much money Mayor Daley received, and they didn't even bother having fund-raiser dinners during his days in office. The money just came in. Where did it come from? From the suppliers, the people who wanted contracts.

Beginning in 1949 or 1950, Senator Paul Douglas of Illinois and Senator William Fulbright of Arkansas held congressional investigations about the dilemmas facing men in the executive branch of government. The hearings were simply descriptive, not accusatory. The senior citizens among us can remember Senators Estes Kefauver and John McClellan, who mesmerized us and educated us on TV. Remember Frank Costello? His lawyer said that his client did not want the camera put on him. So they did not put his face on camera; they focused on his fingers. That, I insist, was part of the beginning of the public's education about what was going on in this country.

In 1960 the New York Bar Association issued a study, "Conflict of Interest in the Federal Services"; in 1970 they issued a companion volume, "Congress in the Public Trust." The studies dealt with the trustee concept of the lawmaker and conflict of interest. These were the years of Bobby Baker and Adam Clayton Powell. All through these years almost every state in the Union passed sets of statutory standards for their public officials. Although I do not wish to say these have been enforced, it is a great step forward to have them at least on the books. But we still have a long way to go.

Why is this? Here are some of the reasons. Many public officials simply make no distinction between private business and working for the government. As far as they are concerned, both are ways of making money. Frequently they get into government because of the leverage they get to promote their own businesses. And we must remember that our public officials receive only part-time compensation. Aldermen, state legislators, many of our commissioners—all are part-time.

But the advances are real. Practices accepted in the past are now being challenged, indeed forbidden. Bribery and extortion are not acceptable. Public attention has focused on conflicts of interest. The Senate Rules Committee in its 1964 investigation of Bobby Baker said "a conflict of interest is deemed by people generally to arise when a public official engages in private business for profit and uses the facilities of his (public) office and his official position to promote and carry on such a business." The fiduciary concept of public office and the statutes based on it incorporate the concept of the public servant as a trustee of the common good, and, to the extent that he uses the common governmental funds for his own private interests, he is in violation of his trust. Thus it seems to me that we are moving toward holding our public officials accountable. There is a famous statement of Senator Dirksen in response to the plea that senators should state their assets. As only Dirksen could do, he rose up in anger and said, "Why, what do you mean? The integrity of the senators has already been established by the voters." That view is passé today.

How as a people are we holding the officials to accountability? Let me tell three ways. First, we are demanding disclosure. Since congressmen are only part-time, congressmen do not find disclosure easy. In 1980 more congressmen chose not to run for re-election than in any other year. The second is divestiture. Public officials are being asked to divest themselves of any assets that would come into conflict with their responsibilities as public officials. The third, toward which we are still groping, is campaign financing. The 1975 statute as interpreted by the Supreme Court in *Buckley* v. *Valeo* has led political action committees and independent committees to certain excesses in contributions to presidential candidates and congressmen. I suggest that we will need to restrict further the use of monies by individuals and by corporations in supporting candidates.

I also suggest that further developments will come about through investigative reporting, through the Freedom of Information Act, through TV coverage, even though it is often distorted, and most of all through a public that is constantly growing more sophisticated. We will continue to be, on the question of ethics in public life, a people in continual transition. But the momentum for change is there and cannot be stopped. Let me conclude with a clipping from yesterday's (March 30) *Tribune*. The headline was: "Top Byrne Donor Gets Another City Auditing Contract." An accounting firm gave $25,000 to Mayor Byrne's political fund in 1980 and has received $200,000 in city business since September. The *Tribune* learned that the firm had been hired to do the audit of the Chicago Park District as well. That means 5 percent has gone to 10 percent. Besides disclosure, divestiture, and campaign financing, this kind of thing may be the next item.

MINISESSION B

Dr. Joyce P. Wexler: Surely you are all familiar with Elizabeth Kübler-Ross and her work with patients in hospitals. One of Kübler-Ross's theories is that we have not humanistically adjusted to the enormous impact of the technology available in hospitals today. Our bodies are treated in the twenty-first century way, but our minds still operate in a very primitive way. One of the problems that patients have in hospitals is that their bodies are treated as machines.

I would like to tell a personal story. My mother-in-law had been very ill. The climax of her illness was a kind of congestive heart failure, and my husband rushed her to the hospital. She was treated in the emergency room. Apparently she "died" on the table but was revived. She was in intensive care. After eight days, my husband went down to the cashier to see what the bill was so far. He asked the cashier what the bill was, and she said to him, "What's the difference? She is on Medicare." He said, "Still I would like to know how much it cost," and she told him that so far the bill came to about $18,000. He said, "My God, what did they do in the days before Medicare?" She said, "We let them die."

May I now present to you Dr. Kerwin Lebeis, a professor in the Department of Psychiatry at the Stritch School of Medicine, who will speak on "The Hospital Patient: Who Cares?"

The Hospital Patient: Who Cares?
Dr. Kerwin Lebeis

This paper describes the firsthand experience of a consulting liaison psychiatrist who investigates care and concern for the patient in the hospital. These observations aim not at explanation but at stimulating further dialogue.

The example given by Dr. Wexler highlights the basic situation. In her short example the miracles of modern technology are contrasted with callousness toward basic human concerns. When the clerk delivered her devastating words, she spoke as only one representative of the entire hospital. Had Dr. Wexler's husband received more direct information from the doctor, the clerk's remark might have been put more into perspective.

How do caring personnel act in a hospital? One way to express care and concern is to foster the patient's sense of identity. By identity I mean not a static state but the direction in which a patient moves in important areas of his life. A person may express his identity in several ways. A man usually selects a mate carefully, choosing someone with whom he has much in common. He is apt to choose a mate who reminds him of his mother. His identity is further defined by his choice of profession and by his values and beliefs. Values and belief systems resist change as if they have a momentum.

Hospital personnel, especially nurses, have the opportunity to express care and concern for patients. The expression may be hidden from a casual observer and may seem to be discouraged by the hierarchy of the professional. Nurses can help reinforce a patient's identity by remembering such data as marital status, occupation, and names of relatives who visit. They may be aware of conflicts or difficulties the patient has with family members. They may understand the patient's emotional reactions and help him ventilate his feelings.

Some younger nurses complain that their superiors rate them in a mechanical way, according to the objective tasks they have completed. The hierarchy ignore any efforts made to acknowledge the identity of patients in the ways listed above. Ratings for nurses do not include their relating to patients as human beings in the hospital. Yet many nurses are committed to showing care and concern for the psychological aspects of patient care. Education provides another avenue to express care and concern.

Values and beliefs are closely connected with medicine and health and may be altered by education. In this paper *education* means verbal and nonverbal messages used by someone in authority to inform others. Many studies show that educational intervention can have a dramatic effect on the course of an illness. For example, one study showed that education of patients prior to cardiac surgery decreased postoperative delirium.[1] Our hospital uses education in this area. Egbert and others have studied the effects of encouragement and instruction on postoperative pain, and they have reached similar conclusions.[2]

Education has been suggested as a means of decreasing disability.[3] The myth that any exertion by a patient with heart disease may lead to sudden death is dangerously misleading and might even, in certain cases, prove crippling. One might consider education by the physician as a moral duty. Education to provide psychological support is often underutilized for patients appropriately eligible for such approaches. What interferes with this approach?

In this age of consumer advocacy, the fears of both doctors and patients ought to be examined. In the experience of both psychiatrists and nonpsychiatrists the simultaneous presence of medical and psychiatric syndromes seems fairly common.[4] While I do not know of any specific description of doctors' reactions to this situation, Kris suggests that patient ambivalence may affect the doctor-patient relationship, if the patient feels a conflict between remaining independent by ignoring his symptoms and becoming dependent by seeking appropriate help.

One hears the question: "How much is organic and how much

is functional?" Semantically and logically we might desire more clarification from this question. In more operational terms, does the psychological state of a patient greatly influence the physical state or vice versa? Margulies and Havens suggest that an initial approach to human dilemmas in psychotherapy would proceed better along interactional and existential lines than along purely logical and rational lines.[6] The same suggestion may apply to dilemmas in the physical-psychological interface.

The training of doctors is either predominantly psychological-behavioral or technical-medical. Training does not cover both realms equally. Because medical technology is so complex and specialized, the young doctor being trained in the technical-medical realm has no time to learn how to manage the behavioral situations that often affect ill persons.

A certain set of behaviors and attitudes is common in doctors trained mostly in the technical-medical realms. The attitude of many of these doctors, even those who have knowledge of psychiatric nomenclature, is that a "crazy" patient needs a "shrink." (These words may be said in a fairly jovial manner.) To these doctors a "shrink" seems to have an easy job compared to the tough job of the practice of technical medicine. As a behavioral-psychological consultant, I find the available interactions with nonpsychiatric physicians to be unacceptable. As a friend of the physician, one may lose leverage; as a psychological consultant, one may be ignored. A no-win situation.

Nonpsychiatric physicians who have not been particularly trained in behavioral interventions with patients can be expected to have uncertainties and anxieties in this area. Usually, clear, direct admissions of these feelings are relatively rare compared with the number of grandiose statements concerning the hardships of the practice of technical medicine. However, I have observed many instances where grandiose attitudes were replaced by sincere gratitude when the consultant simply addressed the underlying anxieties. This dramatic shift in attitude may even occur without directly solving the problem of the patient. Further education of the physician may provide a bit of psychological perspective that the medical specialist lacks.

Patients may also educate their physicians about the psychological aspects of care. But this must be done carefully. Pouring out *all* one's troubles on the first visit to a physician may not prove effective. Over a long period of time, patients had better ask specific questions about how their medical problems may vary according to emotional stress. Also, they had better gently train their physicians to be sensitive to their emotional reactions. Not every physician will find such talk interesting, but alternate physicians exist.

Two common fears patients have can be directly approached in dealing with the physician. Patients may fear that any mention of emotional reaction will mean an automatic label of "crazy" or "crock" or worse. Or they may fear that discussion of nerves may mean that they will not get an adequate, thorough, medical work-up for physical illness. An open approach to these matters, where physician and patient share their concerns, seems desirable.

A patient may be startled and dismayed by the rapid and intense reaction of his physician when behavioral and psychological factors enter the picture. Even physicians who are "psychologically oriented" may have a backlog of heartrending experiences of which their current patients have no knowledge. In the past, patients may have refused diagnostic or treatment methods that the physician considered absolutely vital for the patient's well-being. Or the physician may have been misdirected into overly aggressive diagnostic and treatment methods. Patients should thus be counseled to be patient with their physicians.

In these cases, the approach ought to be to avoid specifying the exact percentage of organic versus psychological. Instead, there should be some recognition that many physicians, psychiatrist as well as nonpsychiatrist, have understandable anxieties. Concurrent psychological and medical problems present difficult situations. Psychiatrists in consultation services have a special obligation to guard against countergrandiosity and arrogance, since they may know more about medical technology than their nonpsychiatric colleagues know about behavioral principles.

Care and concern for hospital patients involves us all. The hospital provides a laboratory in which to observe struggles for health, integrity, and a sense of identity. In these struggles, caring professionals may contribute small but valuable aids as they help patients to correlate physical and emotional reactions. The caring professional ought not to condone arrogance. Instead, the educational process between physician and patient intended to modify dysfunctional beliefs becomes a legitimate and healthy source of pride. The perspective of the team approach allows acknowledgment and awareness of concern on many levels in the hospital system.

Notes

1. C. P. Kimball, "Psychological Responses to the Experience of Open-Heart Surgery I," *American Journal of Psychiatry* 125 (1969): 348-359.

2. L. D. Egbert, G. E. Battit, C. E. Welch, et al., "Reductions of Post-Operative Pain by Encouragement and Instruction of Patients: A Study of Doctor-Patient Rapport," *New England Journal of Medicine* 270 (1964): 825-827.

3. H. S. Moffic and E. S. Paykel, "Depression in Medical In-patients," *British Journal of Psychiatry* 126 (1975): 346.

4. R. C. W. Hall, E. R. Gardner, S. K. Stickney, A. F. LeCann, and M. K. Popkina, "Physical Illness Manifesting as Psychiatric Disease," *Archives of General Psychiatry* 37 (1980): 989-999.

5. K. Kris, "Psychiatric Consultation in the Management of Patient Ambivalence Interfering with the Doctor-Patient Relationship," *American Journal of Psychology* 138, No. 2 (1981): 194.

6. A. Margulies and L. L. Havens, "The Initial Encounter: What to Do First?" *American Journal of Psychiatry* 138, No. 4 (1981): 421-428.

7. R. F. Klein, A. Dean, L. M. Wilson, and M. D. Bogdonoff, "The Physician and Postmyocardial Infarction Invalidism," *Journal of the American Medical Association* 194, No. 2 (1965): 143.

MINISESSION C

Ms. Kim Cavnar: It is my privilege this afternoon to introduce to you Father Bert Akers. He has degrees in political science and philosophy. He has been chairman of the theology department at Scranton University. He was production director for the Sacred Heart radio and TV programs; as such he was responsible for approximately 400 radio and TV programs each week. From 1969 to 1978, Father Akers was the national director of "Jesuits and Communication" in the United States. Currently, besides being an associate professor in the department of communications since 1978 and the director of religious communication at the graduate level since 1979, he is serving on a committee for government regulatory activity, which deals with ethics and accountability in broadcasting. At this point I will turn the floor over to Father Akers.

Circumstances Beyond *Whose* Control?
Father Bert Akers, S.J.

This session of the 1981 Baumgarth Symposium was designed not as a paper but as a series of observations inviting reflection and discussion. But there is a position: we are saying in effect that the present system of mass communication in the United States—especially television—encourages at least by default an ethical vacuum, an irresponsibility highly injurious to the American public; and that furthermore this system, far from being a neutral, value-free technology, consistently and effectively promotes a philosophy of life so total and so closed that it must be likened to an ideology or even a religious faith. It is equally important that we make it clear what we are *not* about: we are critiquing a system, not assessing blame, least of all upon the dedicated and often exceptionally high-principled individuals variously involved with mass communications.

A Modest Disclaimer
The disclaimer itself goes back to broadcasting's age of innocence, when it was still something of a wonder that the night skies were filled with voices, that Montreal (Canada!) came wireless (no wires?) through the walls into the living room, and a symphony orchestra was summoned like a genie from a wooden box. In those days, to those who huddled close, the howls and clicks and crackles told of the weird and preternatural, and powers greater than ourselves dealt whimsically with our Promethean probes at the ionosphere. There were indeed many "circumstances beyond our control."

Less innocent by far, the media themselves these days speak with a kind of higher-state omniscience—when all goes well. But let there be a glitch or a goof (Indira Gandhi captioned as a rock star) and you never heard such a profusion of "What, who, me's?" and pious acknowledgments of one's place in the cosmos, as they trot out the handy old exoneration. Actually, as

93

professionals in the media industries know full well, most problems and difficulties take place, as they say, "between the earphones." Most circumstances, technical and otherwise, are in fact *within* our control, and that should suggest something too about ethical responsibility.

The Presence and the Power

The presence of the media in our lives is a reality too well known and experienced to need verification here. We've all been treated to the statistics in frustrating variations and imposing consistency. The most recent publication of the Office of Consumer Information informs us, for example, that on any given Saturday night one out of every two people in the United States is watching the Tube; and that over 40 percent of Americans rank the TV set as their third most prized possession. (I for one am curious as to what the other two are.) My favorite statistic is that we now spend more time watching TV than in any other human occupation—except sleeping. Its presence we (somewhat guiltily) admit to. Its power we have scarcely begun to acknowledge.

Missing the Ethical Forest

We all experience post-TV depression after those football marathons, disapprove for others (even as our own addiction grows) all that "sex and suffering in the afternoon." We worry about our kids watching too much TV, about junk food, cavity counts, designer jeans. We know we're supposed to be concerned about sex and violence. Exactly what and why are never any too clear. Unfortunately few of these concerns come near to getting at the real questions we need to be asking ourselves about the power of the media and its implications for American society.

Still worse, something of the same selective anonymity, the same uncertainty, perhaps the same immature wish to have it both ways—fully in charge but in no way responsible—occurs in a far more serious area when we touch upon ethical responsibility.

There are howls and growls and crackles in the ethical atmosphere also. And still throughout the industry and among those charged with its regulation (the Congress and the FCC), and among those most deeply affected (the public, ourselves), observing the mess that we have made, we once again invoke the traditional disclaimer: "Due to circumstances beyond our control."

Spore of the Ethical Buck

Again we are not arguing here that any of the "players" involved with the broadcasting industries in the United States are unethical, but that serious structural defects leave accountability and ethical responsibility extremely diffused; so that in practice what is often by its nature an unpleasant burden is left to others, let go by default, or refused out of a popular interpretation of a great but complex principle such as "freedom of speech and of the press."

All the good will in the world (and there is less than that available) will not change the inner dynamics of a *system*. That inner nature will be ignored at one's peril: a toothbrush is not a scalpel. From the earliest days of broadcasting in the United States, the airwaves have been considered a public resource owned by the American people; and the privilege of broadcasting (being the trustee of a frequency of the electromagnetic spectrum) has been directly coupled with the responsibility for serving the "interest, convenience, or necessity" of the American public. Unfortunately this noble principle of the Broadcasting Act of 1934 has now all but eroded, yielding to the far more tangible (and rewarding) demands of commerce and political expediency. In a harsh word, none of the players involved has seen fit to assume ethical responsibility—perhaps, structurally, they cannot be expected to—and, given the structural dynamic, no amount of individual idealism and courage can succeed for long in changing the ethical values that the system represents.

The Congress and the FCC

In the United States the electromagnetic spectrum used for commercial broadcasting is considered a national resource, like parks, forests, and waterways, to be administered by the Congress through its regulatory arm, the Federal Communications Commission. Unfortunately neither of these bodies is very well suited even to regulate the communications industries, let alone to foster positive ethical values. Legislators shrink from venturing over the sacred preserves of freedom of speech and separation of church and state. The mortal sin of secular democracy is known as "imposing one's values"—thereby preserving the

95

schizophrenic myth that majority rule does not do precisely that. But every bit as serious: politicians are absolutely dependent upon the media for election to office and effectiveness in office. All politics is now media politics to a dangerously unrecognized degree. These days it would be hard to decide to whom the term *newsmaker* more aptly applies: the one who does or the one who reports. In any case, such interdependence and congruence of interests make serious ethical challenge predictably rare.

The systemic limitations and concrete historical development of the Federal Communications Commission make its involvement with ethical questions even less promising. Even apart from the current trend towards federal deregulation, the FCC has been notoriously weak in promoting the public interest. Often chosen from the industry itself—and all too often returning to high-salaried positions after their term of government service—their concerns are largely technical and legal, and their own values come to accord closely with those of the industry lobbyists. Most recently, they have practically ceded the field by equating commercial interests with the public interest and all but eliminating the few remaining mechanisms for public accountability.

The Broadcasting Industry

Progressively the industry rejects even in theory the notion of public ownership of the airwaves, their own role as trustee of a public resource, and of course consequent responsibilities. And so they have managed nicely to achieve the best of both worlds: like public utilities, they are a monopoly; at the same time they are in fact a privately owned business whose accountability is to its owners (often far removed from the media world) and whose bottom line is profits.

The criterion of profits determines hirings and firings, and the purchase and sale of franchises. It serves to explain a whole cluster of otherwise maddening questions about why television is the way it is. Basically television is not in the business of serving the public "interest, convenience, or necessity"; it is not primarily in the business of informing or even entertaining. It is in the business of business. It is in the business of selling audiences (us) to sponsors at so much a head.

Hence the underlying consistency in a whole hall-of-mirrors world in which news is not really news but entertainment; where the real commercials are the programs consistently advocating a consumerist view of life, and where the winner of the ratings game (largest viewing audience) will often be what the industry itself describes as the LOB: the Least Objectionable Program.

The Scholars

As the great leveler, death has long since been superseded by television. In fact perhaps nothing so reflects our economic and social status as the manner of our leave-taking, but when it comes to watching television we find that intellectuals are just like everybody else, only more so. They are singled out here—the researchers, the analysts—because they have unwittingly contributed to ethical irresponsibility by lending the name of scholarship to the incredible myth that television has no effect on human behavior. Every so often another study appears, funded in haste and researched at leisure, dealing with the effects of television on human behavior and arriving at the astonishing conclusion that there are none.

Is it even conceivable that ruthlessly cost-competitive corporations in this country alone throw away ten billion green ones a year on advertising that has no effect on human behavior? Believe me, these industries have researchers of their own. They know both our rising up and our sitting down. But do we need statistical tables to remind us who taught the world, if not to sing in perfect harmony, at least to guzzle, gargle, plop and fizz, spell *relief* with a *d,* and for that matter stay sweet and dry on commencement day beneath the gowns of academia?

In fairness, what these cautious researchers should say is that they cannot "prove" a cause-effect relationship, allowing no other explanation, between stimulus and response. Whether the methodology used is appropriate to begin with, whether human behavior lends itself to "scientific" verification of this sort is a deep and serious question. When we move from the level of the empirical/descriptive to that of the normative/ethical—from the *is* to the *ought*—it is clear how inadequate our tools are, be they common sense or computerized research, for dealing with the *ethical* implications of the single most powerful force in contemporary society.

A Closed System

Ideology has become an eight-letter word. *Faith* is also not very "nice" in the sense implied here—meaning that nobody (who is anybody) is supposed to have any faith. Of course, and of necessity, everybody does. It is impossible for a human being not to have *some* place to stand, mentally as well as physically: some ultimate belief-system, value-system, reward-system which can and should be reflected upon from time to time, but which is not incessantly questioned and always in the shop awaiting re-assembly. The first principles of intellect, good manners, science, or libertarianism are all held largely as a faith.

What we are suggesting here, without the opportunity to develop the suggestion at length, is that the gravest mistake of all is to view modern media, television especially, merely as a technology—and a neutral one at that. Apart from the fact that no technology is ever neutral (the very existence of a telephone or a sewer-pipe says a great deal), modern television is actually a system. It is upon examination a surprisingly closed system. While it undoubtedly opens up marvelous opportunities for knowledge, information, travel, experience, and so on, it will be found upon examination to promote a philosophy of life that is altogether unoriginal, flattened, and circumscribed.

Lesser evils would include the endorsement given to time-wasting, escapism, fantasizing, game-playing, vicarious living, and spectatorism. More serious and predominant are commercialism and consumerism: identity, status, success, happiness are all purchasable commodities. Most harmful of all: the trivialization of life, the refusal to challenge, to disturb, to deal with, to ask the hard questions, to deal with the ultimate realities, or for that matter to question the condescending arrogance ("And that's the way it is." Really?) of the media industries themselves. Well, at least that's the way it's going to be until we recognize our own ethical responsibility and do something about it.

That is why we have not discussed the ethical responsibility of the most important player of all: the public, ourselves. That, we hope, is what our discussion will lead to.

By Way of Summary

—The power of contemporary media is still largely and dangerously unrecognized;

—the media are not a value-free technology but a business whose bottom line is profits;

—the usual concerns (e.g., about sex and violence) are largely irrelevant to the really serious ethician and moral issues;

—it is the system (rather than individuals) that both violates public rights and fosters unaccountability;

—the present system promotes a philosophy of life so total, so closed that it can only be likened to an ideology or a faith;

—given that system, it will devolve upon an exasperated public to reassume its ethical responsibility and reestablish as an operative criterion the public "interest, convenience, or necessity."

THIRD GENERAL SESSION
Dr. Andrew McKenna
Dr. Paul Breidenbach
Father William Ellos, S.J.
(from left to right)

Underdeveloped Mythology: A Shroud for Global Justice

Dr. Paul S. Breidenbach
Department of Anthropology

Moderator
Dr. Andrew J. McKenna
Department of Modern Languages

Responder
Father William J. Ellos, S.J.
Department of Philosophy

Dr. McKenna: I wish to welcome you to this session of the Baumgarth Symposium on Values and Ethics at Loyola University of Chicago. My name is Andrew McKenna of the Department of Modern Languages.

After reading the essay which I have been asked to introduce to you, I am tempted to open this session with one of my favorite quotes from Baudelaire, that "incorrigible Catholic," as he called himself:

> The World is coming to an end ("Le monde va finir"—The world is drawing to a close). . . . We shall furnish a new example of the inexorability of the spiritual and moral laws and shall be their new

victims: we shall perish by the very thing by which we fancy that we live. Technocracy will Americanize us, progress will starve our spirituality so far that nothing of the bloodthirsty frivolous or unnatural dreams of the utopists will be comparable to those positive facts. (*Fusées,* XV)

Baudelaire's prophecy has deep affinities with those of Jeremiah (9:3-6), with which I won't detain you. For I decided to sound a more positive note with the remarks of another French writer, who is nonetheless Jewish in fact: Claude Lévi-Strauss. This is from his *Tristes tropiques* (sometimes translated as *World on the Wane*):

> Other societies are perhaps no better than our own; even if we are inclined to believe they are, we have no method at our disposal for proving it. However, by getting to know them better, we are enabled to detach ourselves from our own society. Not that our own society is peculiar or absolutely bad. But it is the only one from which we have a duty to free ourselves: we are, by definition, free in relation to the others. We thus put ourselves in a position to embark on the second stage, which consists in using all societies—without adopting features from any one of them—to elucidate principles of social life that we can apply in reforming our own customs and not those of foreign societies: through the operation of a prerogative which is the reverse of the one just mentioned, the society we belong to is the only society we are in a position to transform without any risk of destroying it, since the changes, being introduced by us, are coming from within the society itself. . . . If men have always been concerned with only one task—how to create a society fit to live in— the forces which inspired our distant ancestors are also present in us. Nothing is settled; everything can still be altered. What was done, but turned out wrong, can be done again. "The Golden Age, [as Rousseau stated] which blind superstition had placed behind [or ahead of] us, is *in us.*" The brotherhood of man acquires a concrete meaning when it makes us see, in the poorest tribe, a confirmation of our own image and an experience, the lessons of which we can assimilate, along with so many others. We may even discover a pristine freshness in these lessons. Since we know that, for thousands of years, man has succeeded only in repeating himself, we will attain to that nobility of thought which consists in going back beyond all the repetitions and taking as the starting-point of our reflections the indefinable grandeur of man's beginnings. (Translated by John and Doreen Weightman [New York: Atheneum, 1973], pp. 392-393.)

And so we begin with the paper of Professor Paul Breidenbach of the Department of Anthropology, "Underdevelopment Mythology: A Shroud for Global Justice." After a short response by Professor William Ellos of the Philosophy Department, the discussion will be opened to the audience.

Underdeveloped Mythology:
A Shroud for Global Justice
Dr. Paul S. Breidenbach

Let us imagine for a moment that numerous Loyola security personnel came bursting through the doors of this auditorium and forcibly ejected some of you. Suppose justification for this action was the charge that those expelled were too primitive and unsophisticated to contribute to this event. Or imagine again that an organized and powerful minority, say 30 percent of this audience, were able to bar the 70 percent majority from the hall until 80 percent of this paper had been delivered, and then arbitrarily readmitted them for the remaining 20 percent of the presentation.

Such acts of injustice would be evident and seem outrageous to all of us. Why? Our common involvement in this situation is direct and immediate. We would experience concern because blatant violations of social rights, bonds, and standards, which we take for granted, had occurred. Our sense of outrage would be intensified by the fact that these power plays appear as whims on the part of a minority who give no social or rational justification for their manipulation of the majority. If such unlikely events occurred, an urgent communal outcry demanding that justice be restored would probably ensue and perhaps have an effect.

Now let us shift our attention from this present situation to the much broader context conjured up by the term *global*. Justice in Flanner Hall and justice on planet Earth seem realities of entirely separate and different orders. The definition and administration of justice here and now are manageable and necessary.

Global justice, by contrast, seems an abstract and remote prospect, generally beyond our control. If we have real responsibilities and real bonds that link us to the rest of humankind, they are not as obvious as the ones that bind us to our fellows in this auditorium.

I contend that indeed our links to the rest of humankind are quite real but are not obvious, because we are unwilling to distance ourselves from a comfortable but dangerously myopic, and therefore limited, characterization of these links and bonds. I would like to develop this idea first by considering the extent of injustice in the global distribution of the essential human resources of food and energy. Right now 80 percent of the world's protein is consumed by a powerful and organized minority of 30 percent of the world's people.[1] In regard to protein consumption the 70 percent majority of humankind are in the same position as our 70 percent who were barred from the hall: they get what is left after the majority has satisfied their wants. We in the United States make up less than 7 percent of the global population, yet our complex technoeconomic system requires a disproportionate 35 percent of the world's energy resources to maintain itself.[2] We take this apparent energy need as our rightful due. Some among us propose even more energy-requiring growth as a form of salvation from our own economic woes.[3] From a limited ethnocentric perspective, our participation in the world protein monopoly and energy monopoly is simply the realistic and necessary means of getting what we need. From a global vantage point the growth of and participation in such monopolies appear as contributing factors to the creation of worldwide inequity and injustice.

It has been argued that our advantageous position in regard to food and energy is the direct outcome of our high level of agricultural, technological, and general economic development. The majority of humankind has a smaller portion of the world's food and energy pie because they have not yet caught up with us and other fully industrialized peoples. Systems of food production and energy exploitation in the so-called Third World countries look primitive and unsophisticated when compared to our own; they are underdeveloped. This observation is limited, because it underscores only the obvious advantages of development, ignoring the negative side effects on ourselves and the wider global community and environment. It also obscures the actual historical relationship between the industrialized powers and the "others" of the world by drawing a sharp distinction between "us" and "them," the developed and underdeveloped. This distinction conveniently sets us apart from these other peoples. It also avoids specifying what our actual relationship to them has been and still is. It is an important omission, because this relationship has involved direct and unjust manipulation and subjugation of these peoples as well as less evident common bonds.

Because it relates to my topic of underdevelopment mythology, I need to comment on what I mean by the negative side effects of development in the areas of food and energy. We are familiar with the gain resulting from the American system of agribusiness, abundant supplies of food. This abundance results from a combination of good farmland, intensive use of mechanized farm equipment, chemical fertilizers, and pesticides. Because our transportation and marketing systems are also mechanized, foodstuffs can be quickly moved, processed, packaged, and in some cases chemically preserved for later use. It appears that this system represents a peak of rational efficiency and advance because of its immediate results.

Now let us look at this mode of food production from a comparative and global vantage point afforded by the food production systems devised by other human groups. A. J. Voelker, a British agricultural scientist assigned to India during the 1890s, wrote about the intense rationality and efficiency of the Indian farming system in the following terms:

> Nowhere would one find better instances of keeping land scrupulously clean from weeds, of ingenuity in device of water-raising appliances, of knowledge of soils and their capabilities, as well as the exact time to sow and reap, as one would find in Indian agriculture. It is wonderful too, how much is known of rotation, the system of mixed crops and fallowing. . . . I, at least, have never seen a more perfect picture of cultivation.[4]

Systems of peasant agriculture around the world all attest to the truth of the Chinese proverb that "the best fertilizer is the shadow of the peasant upon the soil." Peasant farming is highly rational and efficient, and its energy requirements are low. Peasant farming is also ecologically sound. The use of animal rather than chemical fertilizers perpetuates a more natural ecological cycle with a minimal polluting effect. It is a time-tested human adaptation that has proven its long-term advantages.[5]

If we take peasant systems as a standard of rationality, efficiency, and ecological wisdom, our system looks exotic and even irrational. Its guiding principle now appears in a different light. It is not based on efficiency at all, but rather on convenience for the consumer and profit for the marketeers. If it were based on efficiency, how could we tolerate the waste that seems to be built into the system? Some years as much as 75 percent of our grain crop is reinvested as food for cattle. This accounts for our participation in the world protein monopoly, but it is not very efficient in terms of the energy it requires. It takes twenty pounds of vegetable protein and added chemicals to produce one pound of United States beef.[6] Is this rational efficiency? No, it is the satisfaction of a cultural food preference which, like other food preferences and cultural taboos, has a merely cultural basis. If our system were rational, how could we tolerate the polluting effects of that dynamic duo of chemical fertilizer and pesticides, not to mention the harm that our heavy equipment does to our precious soil? Consider the global energy drain that our system requires, in the face of declining energy sources, and you will see that rationality and efficiency play little part in our system of food production.

One thing we can learn by shifting to a global and ecological perspective on our own system, so that we can see it as having the same destructive potential as an organized minority on the rampage in this auditorium, is that low-energy systems are more beneficial to the common good of the global community than are high-energy systems. Nonpolluting systems contribute more than polluting ones. We may actually be living now off the good graces provided by the widespread existence of low-energy peasant economies. If all peasants would suddenly reach the state of development that we have reached, with its attendant side effects, we would be facing not an energy crisis but an energy collapse as well as total ecological disaster. Yet still, because we do not really understand the full implications of development, we have started this process along the way by perhaps unconsciously destroying our own earlier reliance on low-energy production as well as many other low-energy systems throughout the world.

106

Now to help us look at how the actual relationship that we have to the others in the world has been obscured, I would like to explain just what I mean by underdevelopment mythology. Myth is a fiction to which reality is true. Vital myth coincides with lived experience. In fictional form it accurately reveals and interprets the truths which a given people have discovered. But human beings stretch mythological explanations to fit domains that often stand beyond their own experience. Myth then becomes an unfounded projection. It gives to its projectors a comfortable sense of comprehension regarding what is really unknown or remote. It is a mode of objectification, but it does not rest on any real or deep-seated contact with reality, which is, via the mythic projection, made to seem objective.

I contend that the term *underdeveloped,* in its popular usage as an adjective describing a group of people, is often no more than a mythic projection whose main function is to give a sense of comprehension and comfort to those who use it. The term does not describe the real-life situation or historical circumstances of those it seems to designate. Rather it obscures that situation and history by adherence to development as the single standard for evaluation. Deviance from this standard mythically substitutes for description.

Since most of us by and large have had little actual contact with the other people in the world who have been designated as underdeveloped, we tend to objectify them in this mythic fashion. Because of the vast differences that are supposed to exist between developed and underdeveloped people, the underlying human term *people* is obscured. These people then appear as distant and different objects. The term *underdeveloped* handles and packages them so that it is hard to see how we are linked to them and they to us. The mythic projection of underdevelopment therefore functions as a shroud for our development of a sense of global justice.

I first became aware of this tendency to obscure our actual relatedness to Third World peoples (another objectifying term) by relying on mythic projection while teaching Anthropology 102 here at Loyola. In a segment of this course entitled "Anthropology and Current Global Problems," questions and responses of my students revealed a heavy reliance on projective explanation. Most were totally unfamiliar with the peoples and types of unjust manipulations that were under discussion. The discussions centered on case studies done by applied anthropologists as they carried out fieldwork in nonindustrial or partially industrialized countries. Let me outline briefly two such case studies, both involving the food and energy issues, to point out how inappropriate the development/underdevelopment dichotomy really is, and how it functions to obscure the actual historical relationship we have had with the others of the world.

The Turtle People

The Miskito Indians, known as the Turtle People, live on the Eastern coast of Nicaragua. Anthropologist Brian Weiss has investigated their indigenous subsistence economy, which was founded on the principle of reciprocal exchange. One segment of the community grew root crops and grain, and another fished for giant sea turtles; these commodities were communally exchanged. Thus all Miskito had access to a balanced diet including protein-rich turtle meat. In recent years the Turtle People have been drawn into the orbit of a worldwide industrial economy based on cash and wage labor.

During Weiss's fieldwork, a North American company that processed and sold turtle soup for the gourmet market in Europe and the United States contacted the Miskito. The fishermen were encouraged to bring in the sea turtles en masse for a payment of $80 per turtle. The company wanted as many turtles as possible since, unlike the Indians who used all the meat, they only used prime portions to produce a gourmet delight. These events had an immediate impact on local diet. Now, distributing the meat did not pay. Agriculture was disrupted since the farmers too began fishing. The energy-intensive fishing, from motorized company boats, led to another of those small ecological disasters we have come to expect in the modern world. The turtle population was decimated. The soup company disappeared, looking for new territories to exploit. The Miskito were left with an impoverished diet, the victims rather than the beneficiaries of "progress." Another small culture had been chewed up and then spit out again in a boom-and-bust cycle initiated by a powerful and organized industrial economic system.[7]

The Sisalaland Farmers

The Sisala are a group of subsistence-level agriculturalists in the northern portion of the West African country of Ghana.

Though Ghana achieved political independence from Great Britain in 1957, its economic dependency on a single colonial cash crop, cocoa, which was subject to the fluctuations of the world market, put the country in a curious position. Since most of the peasant and tribal economies, which were geared to local subsistence needs, had been destroyed in the colonial era, food for local consumption had to be imported. Until 1960 the Sisala had escaped this new plantation economy, which had engulfed their southern neighbors. With a simple technology they provided enough food for themselves, growing yams, beans, and other food crops. Anthropologist Eugene Mendonsa, who lived among the Sisala in 1974-75, has described how the introduction of modern farming techniques put the Sisala in a situation of hunger and dependency.

After independence, Great Britain, the United States, and the Soviet Union descended upon the new nation in order to help them solve their food problems—which were ironically the result of intervention by outside colonial forces. They argued that development was the answer. These nations competed to sell Ghana tractors, chemical fertilizers, pesticides, and any other technology required for development. Under the pressure of these arguments, local elites who were committed to this sort of development (with its attendant profits) made self-sufficiency through modernized agriculture a high priority. The Sisala were convinced that tractors were the answer. Then OPEC prices began to rise. We felt this energy crunch in the United States but could still compete for scarce and costly resources. Ghana was not able to compete. By 1975 no gasoline could be found in Sisalaland to run the shiny new tractors. And if gasoline had been available, no Sisala farmer could have paid the price required. The subsistence economy of the Sisala, which could have fed them, was no longer functional and the modernized economy required unavailable energy. The result was once again local misery and starvation.[8]

When confronted with these case studies, my students quickly glossed over the role that outside manipulation and the fostering of dependency relationships played in bringing about an inadequate diet for one people and starvation for another. They said that the Sisala and the Miskito suffered because they were underdeveloped people. I asked what this term meant to them. They replied that it meant that these peoples were shortsighted, unorganized, too traditional, and they lacked the initiative to better themselves by competitive effort. In short, they *did not* possess modern attitudes. The situation was thus mythically explained, not in terms of the actual dominance and submission relationship that was at work, but by invoking development as a criterion of judgment and then finding none. Thus lack of development stands as an explanation for Third World misery. In this world of mythic analysis the issue of justice or injustice is never raised, because the underlying dominance and submission relationship is not addressed, as it would be addressed if such events occurred here and now.

In her initial research into the causes of world hunger, Frances Lappé, author of *Diet for a Small Planet,* held a view not too far removed from that of my students. She notes that, before deeper research, she saw:

> a world divided into two parts, a minority of nations that had "taken off" through their agricultural and industrial revolutions to reach an unparalleled material abundance, and a majority that remained behind in a primitive, traditional, and underdeveloped state. This lagging behind of the majority of the world's peoples must be due . . . to some internal deficiency or even several of them. It seemed obvious that the underdeveloped countries must be deficient in natural resources, particularly good land and climate, and in cultural development, including modern attitudes conducive to work and progress.[9]

An intensive study of Western colonialism and neocolonialism, which focused on the relationship between the colonizer and the colonized and the demands made on nonindustrial countries, led Lappé to radically different conceptions of underdevelopment:

> I learned that my picture of these two separate worlds was false. My two separate worlds were really just different sides of the same coin. One side was on top *because* the other side was on the bottom. . . . I saw that colonialism had destroyed the cultural patterns of production and exchange by which traditional societies in underdeveloped countries had previously met the needs of the people. Many precolonial social structures . . . had evolved a system of mutual obligation which helped insure at least a minimal diet for all. Underdeveloped became for me a verb (to underdevelop) meaning the process by which the minority of the world has transformed— indeed often robbed and degraded—the majority.[10]

The cases of the Miskito and Sisala are vivid and concrete illustrations of the nonmythical view of underdevelopment that Lappé arrived at. In each case a viable subsistence economy was destroyed by the intervention of an industrial power which totally ignored the local needs of the local people. In both cases the representative entrepreneurs of the industrial power, if asked, would probably say that they were not exploiting but rather bringing development into a formerly backward area. But let's not ask them! Let's ask the Miskito and the Sisala! They could tell us of the actual results: injustice, misery, dependence on an unsupportable and overly exploitative technology, and a poorer diet than before the developers arrived. The Europeans and Americans who contacted these people did not discover an underdeveloped people, they created an underdeveloped people. This type of underdevelopment, as an ongoing process, widens the gap between the rich and poor peoples of the world more and more as each day passes.

While underdevelopment mythology obscures the exploitative relationship we have had with the remote others of the world, it also obscures the growing common bond which could bring us together with them in a more harmonious relationship. One of the greatest sources of human solidarity has always been a common threat, existence in the same precarious situation. We are all faced with the first fruits of the real situation, which is one of overdevelopment: inordinate energy requirements and finite dwindling resources, ecological imbalances which are not confined to any country but are related to a global ecological system. The communicative systems that now link us to the remote corners of the world need not function merely as channels by which we are informed of the latest political crisis or ecological disaster. They have a potential for real communication in a time of common planetary crisis. We might even learn something about low-energy and nonpolluting modes of subsistence from those people who still practice them. Peasant and tribal ideologies of reciprocal exchange and communal sharing of limited resources are attitudes that modernized cultures, alienated in their own situation of overdevelopment and backfiring mastery of the environment, could use with profit.

Much of what I have said up to this point gives a somewhat pessimistic image of our planet, as though it has been merely an arena for a global chess game of strategic and economic advantage, a game that results in pollution, destruction, and injustice. The world at times does appear to me as being like a circus ring in which overdeveloped elephants dance around crushing the less powerful chickens who are in the ring with them. At the same time I have also pointed out that if we can see beyond the myths surrounding both development and underdevelopment, there are common bonds and situational circumstances that bind the chickens to the elephants and the elephants to the chickens. Both need a world that is fit for human habitation, that promotes harmony and exchange, while tolerating the diversity of cultural and economic adaptations, and particularly low-energy adaptations, that currently exist. This in my view would be a world of global justice.

What role does the Loyola community have in promoting the recognition of underlying human unity and common human needs as well as the emergence of such a world of global justice? First, it has the role of any university community, to develop in its members skills leading to critical and informed awareness of our own society and the wider world. This process of consciousness raising takes place in a confrontation with our own longstanding traditions of cultural wisdom, which we cannot afford to accept uncritically, as well as up-to-date knowledge of the larger global context. Here at Loyola we have some of the tools and resources to further demythologize the underdevelopment myth; we have the opportunity to investigate the remote others of the world and make their plight less remote to us. We have the opportunity to participate in an interdisciplinary course which investigates world hunger, the global food crisis, and the alternative solutions that have been proposed regarding this critical problem.

As an anthropologist I would naturally prefer to see a greater emphasis in this university on essential information about peoples and cultures who stand outside the Euro-American tradition. These people constitute the majority of humankind. We need to further authentically global perspectives on the study of human problems of injustice through the study of non-Western culture and history as well as the history of European and American colonialism. We no longer live in the nineteenth century when one could be comforted by the fact that a great divide seemed to separate "the West from the rest." Nor can we be blinded by the nineteenth-century ideology that rested on a vision of unending and unlimited industrial expansion taken as a sign of progress in the realms of morality and happiness. Looking at other cultures on their own terms, with their alternative views of how to relate to the planet without vast outlays of energy, is the surest way to avoid the ethnocentric attitudes that lead to reliance on mythic projection as a spurious sort of understanding.

My own fieldwork experience in Ghana has given me a perspective that I now cherish, the viewpoint of the other that comes with the attempt at detachment from one's own cultural tradition insofar as this is possible. The cases of the Sisala and the Miskito were used to convey this viewpoint to my students. Yet their total unfamiliarity with these types of cultures made it difficult. Direct contact with non-Western peoples and the exploitative situations in which they find themselves is the best cure for ethnocentrism. Still most of you will never travel to Nicaragua or Ghana. You have to fill this gap in experience with the kind of knowledge of the peoples of the world that you will acquire here at Loyola. We can ask ourselves today if the extent to which this type of knowledge is stressed at Loyola is proportionate to the need that we have for it and the critical importance of the issues of global justice that could be clarified by it.

Knowledge is essential, but it is not enough; and Loyola is more than a university. It is a Jesuit and a Catholic university. Critical attitudes should not be fostered amidst an ethical vacuum. We hope to promote ethical concern that is enlivened by the relevance of the Catholic faith to the widest possible context in which human affairs are conducted. Membership in the Catholic church is another real link to the rest of the world. In respect to the issue of social justice, in many Third World countries, this Church has recently been both vocal and active regarding the relevance of its teachings. Catholicism has a long tradition of thought relating to social justice. Too often in the past this tradition has been "hidden under a bushel." The church has at various times and places been identified, not with the oppressed, but with the interests of those engaged in colonial subjugation of the type described by Lappé. The rise of new movements, such as that of liberation theology in Latin America, indicates that the church will no longer sit back and let powerful minorities work their will on powerless majorities.[11]

Reactions of combined social and ethical concern on the part of the Church arise from a firsthand exposure to human misery and degradation so common in the poorer nations of the world. Representatives of the Church, many of them nationals of the countries involved, see each day the results of the unjust manipulation of their people by corporate economic interest groups and greedy local elites. They experience processes that are by and large hidden from us. What is remote to us is not remote to them. They relate to people not as underdeveloped others but as fellows caught up in a common situation, much as we are in a common situation today in this auditorium. Our bonds with these people may not be as direct, but they are nonetheless real. Looking beyond the veil of the mythology that has obscured this real bond, let's ask ourselves as individuals and members of this community what we can do, not only to recognize this relationship, but to strengthen it.

Notes

1. Alan S. Miller, *A Planet to Choose* (New York: Pilgrim Press, 1978), p. 1.

2. Ibid.

3. The economic policies proposed by the Reagan administration, for example, are based on out-of-date notions of economic progress. I say that they are out of date because they ignore the negative side effects on other world populations that our past industrial expansion required. Closer to home, this administration seems willing to sacrifice the already inadequate gains we have made in energy conservation and ecological consciousness. This is not to mention the general retreat from social programs, which while imperfect in their implementation, have indicated at least some commitment to people rather than the production of objects for corporate profit. The administration justifies greater economic growth because it will "put people back to work" and "reactivate" our economy. They assert that we can do all of this by greater reliance on our own energy resources (which, like global resources, are finite). This "solution" omits one important detail. Most of the economic problems we have in the United States today are merely symptoms of wider global problems. Inflation, unemployment, and scarce and costly resources and energy are global problems. National economic revitalization programs that almost totally ignore the global economic order seem in my view doomed to failure. They are well grounded in the nineteenth-century myth that a nation is a fully independent entity that must act only in terms of its own self-interest.

4. Radha Sinha, *Food and Poverty* (New York: Holmes & Meier, 1976), p. 26.

5. Anthropologist Marvin Harris provides us with a clear-cut demonstration of these propositions. He adopts an ecological perspective when contrasting development in India, whose economy is still largely grounded in the peasant mode of production, and in the United States. He responds to the idea that the Indian practice of taboo on eating sacred cows is backward. He shows that it is ecologically sound. The cows produce bullocks which operate as low-energy tractors in the Indian system. If they were slaughtered for immediate food, an ecological disaster would occur, because India could not replace them at this point with high-energy technology. If India could do this, it would be facing the same energy demands we face, which are in the long run unsupportable. Harris notes that efficiency and rationality are not the basis of industrial development, as many think. In large part, industrial development rests upon a high level of energy waste. I cite here the concluding paragraph of his article "Mother Cow." "The higher standard of living enjoyed by the industrial nations is not the result of greater productive efficiency, but of an enormously expanded increase in the amount of energy available per person. In 1970, the United States used up the energy equivalent of twelve tons of coal per inhabitant, while the corresponding figure for India was one-fifth ton per inhabitant. The way this energy was expended involved far more energy being wasted per person in the United States than in India. Automobiles and airplanes are faster than ox carts, but they do not use energy more efficiently. In fact, more calories go up in useless heat and smoke during a single day of traffic jams in the United States than is wasted by all the cows of India during an entire year. The comparison is even less favorable when we consider the fact that the stalled vehicles are burning up irreplaceable reserves of petroleum that it took the earth tens of millions of years to accumulate. If you want to see a real sacred cow, go out and look at the family car." Marvin Harris, *Cows, Pigs, Wars, and Witches* (New York: Vintage Books, 1974), pp. 26-27.

6. John H. Bodley, *Anthropology and Contemporary Human Problems* (Menlo Park, Calif.: Cummings, 1976), p. 125.

7. Daniel R. Gross, "Review of *The Turtle People,* Brian Weiss," *The American Anthropologist* 76 (1974): 487. An ethnographic film, made by Weiss, called "The Turtle People," demonstrates this exploitation of the Miskito. It is available from the Audiovisual Services of Pennsylvania State University.

8. Eugene L. Mendonsa, "The Failure of Farming in Sisala-land, Northern Ghana," *Human Organization* 39, No. 3 (Fall 1980): 275.

9. Frances Moore Lappé, "Why Can't People Feed Themselves?" in *Readings in Anthropology: Annual Editions 1980-81* (Guilford, Conn.: Dushkin Publishing Group), p. 214.

10. Ibid.

11. Avery Dulles, S.J., "The Meaning of Faith Considered in Relationship to Justice" in *The Faith That Does Justice,* ed. John C. Haughey (New York: Paulist Press, 1977), pp. 11-12.

Underdevelopment Mythology: A Shroud for Global Injustice
A Response by Father William J. Ellos, S.J.

Central to Doctor Breidenbach's presentation is his use of two myths in the understanding of the world. The first of these myths is the developed/underdeveloped myth in which certain nations are taken to be developed so they may with impunity operate somewhat ruthlessly on underdeveloped nations, because these nations are not in the same category as developed nations. The underdeveloped nations exist only or primarily to be worked on or developed, not to develop themselves. The second myth is the dominance/dependence myth. Quoting Frances Lappé with approbation, Dr. Breidenbach says that one group of nations is on top because the other group is on the bottom. He then goes on to suggest that we must really demythologize both of these myths. This we must do because the world community is now such a global village that no such dichotomizing myths can possibly be maintained in the face of our complete and total interdependence. While the demythologizing is basically correct, it might well be important to linger for a few moments on the two myths because, as in all myths, part of what is claimed is indeed true and part false.

In considering the developed/underdeveloped myth, for example, Dr. Breidenbach maintains that Europeans and Americans who contacted primitive people did not discover an underdeveloped people; they created an underdeveloped people. There are multiple problems here. First of all, the use of the terms *developed* and *underdeveloped* will vary depending on the point of view one takes. The primal peoples did not consider themselves underdeveloped. It is not surprising that an anthropologist would be highly sensitive to this view. And certainly we would never say they are culturally underdeveloped. Yet from the point of view of the colonizer, they really are underdeveloped in many areas other than the strictly cultural. So there is a real moral obligation for the developed nations to provide better medicine, better methods of education, better methods of farming, and in many cases better social and political organization. An equating of a lack of culture with a lack of these basic goods and services is certainly incorrect, and to maintain that simply because a culture is not underdeveloped, other areas of its life are also not underdeveloped, causes serious miscalculation of what should be done in critical situations.

For example, the idyllic cultural life of the Indian peasant is rightly lauded, but one should not then go on to say that such a culture will be able to provide food and medicine to India's millions, which it most obviously does not. Here, instead of rejecting the development/underdevelopment myth, we should embrace and use it so that we really can bring the help so urgently needed. When this help is given, however, some rather serious problems arise, because any catering to these disparate material and social needs will bring about in the culture changes of a serious and lasting nature. Hence in the case of the turtle fishermen or the introduction of tractors in Ghana, it can seem as though the developed nation is consciously trying to manipulate and change the depth culture, when really it is catering to more pressing needs of the surface culture, in this case the need for the fishermen to earn a more decent wage and for the farmers to produce more food. At the root of the problem seems to be the very use of the developed/underdeveloped myth model, as any use of such a model will inevitably lead us first of all to make false dichotomies and then to operate with a false analysis of what actually occurs. Especially our analysis of the results tends to deal with the surface practical details of the immediate consequences of the developed/underdeveloped roles rather than a deeper study and awareness of the more significant cultural dimensions. We might better focus our attention on these depth cultural values, differing in their surface manifestations, but common to both so-called developed and underdeveloped societies.

The second myth which must be examined and then rejected is the dominance/dependency myth. According to this myth, strong and powerful colonial powers went into areas where they saw that they could very profitably exploit the local situation so as to set up an economic dependency. Part of this myth is indeed true, but also a fair amount of it must be understood as simply a quite healthy symbiotic relationship between the rich and the poor country. Raw materials, which otherwise were bringing no wealth either to the poor or the rich country while they lay in the ground or remained unharvested, brought a certain amount of wealth to both the rich and the poor country. However, the longer the colonial situation tended to go on, the more real exploitation undoubtedly occurred; the mother country often laid down harsh tariff laws or required that the manufacturing be done there rather than in the colony. Eventually injustice and oppression resulted. But just as we saw in the developed/underdeveloped myth, not all in the dominance/dependency myth is wrong. What might well be done is to resituate the two myths in a context that would preserve what is true, correct, and useful in the actual situations.

Toward the end of his paper Professor Breidenbach suggests that since all nations, rich and poor, are now bound together, we must develop a new and radically different mythology. He suggests that this mythology might have a religious base in some sort of theological movement such as liberation theology. The remainder of these comments will try to propose such a new mythology, which hopefully in a religious context will provide a more secure and fruitful model than have the two previous mythologies.

It is most helpful to use the contributions of anthropology in understanding how integral and important to any culture a good and solid mythology is. We might take the work of the eminent French anthropologist, Claude Lévi-Strauss, as an example. Lévi-Strauss maintains that any really strong mythology has a surface, linear, or diachronic aspect. That is to say, if we view any of the aspects of a culture on the surface level, we would note a somewhat bewildering variety of seemingly disparate elements. If a visitor from Carl Sagan's deep space were, for instance, to land in Chicago at Christmas, he, she, or it would encounter cribs, Christ-figures, Santas, elves, dwarfs, reindeer, Hanukkah cards, prodigious varieties of intense sales pitches, tinsel, fir trees, yule logs, snowmen, and on and on. These are all surface elements of vast complexity. It would make no sense at all until the visitor went deeper and realized that this is a celebration of a Christian and a Jewish feast along with a heavy dose of mercantilism filtered through German, French, English, and many other national customs and spliced together by such cultural geniuses as Marshall Field and Sears.

The depth, unchanging elements are termed by Lévi-Strauss axial, synchronic factors. These do not change in the course of time but remain the secure deep base of action.

Any really solid myth must have both a tremendous variety of surface, changeable elements and some changeless depth values, which guide and give meaning to the seemingly bewildering surface array. As regards economic factors, the developed/underdeveloped and the dominance/dependence factors might both be noted to be surface phenomena of the economic scene. Thus they make no sense on their own, but must be apprehended as underpinned by deeper perennial values and truths.

The deepest truths to which we adhere are usually religious values and truths, and here in various forms of theological reasoning we attempt to apply these deep matters to the complexity, in this case, of economic development. Christianity maintains that through all the complexities of life, including economic life, there is a deep and abiding presence of God in Jesus Christ, which remains the same no matter what occurs to individuals or to nations. Thus the really deep, Christian, synchronic, axial values stress that economics and money are very much surface things with no real value unless they are anchored in the poverty of the God-man Jesus. Hence the constant identification of Christianity with poverty, making it difficult for the Christian to commit himself to the elimination of all poverty, as Christ tells us that it is the key to deep religious understanding. If all economic systems in the world are at their very worst, the Christian is still synchronically anchored in the values of the poor Christ.

Judaism, on the other hand, is much committed to the betterment of the human condition, so that according to our analysis of myth, Judaism shows a much more surface, linear, diachronic approach. Deuteronomy, Leviticus, Isaiah, Jeremiah, and much of the Wisdom literature are concerned in often minute detail with the political and economic amelioration of the human condition and make this amelioration an important condition of reconciliation with God. (The biblical material on poverty in the Old and the New Testament can best be looked up in John L. McKenzie's *Dictionary of the Bible* [Milwaukee: Bruce Publishing Co., 1965], pp. 681-684.)

As a result, when we look through the most common Western religious traditions, we see an emphasis now on the surface, now on the depth levels in dealing with economic issues. It is then no surprise that there is debate about the merits and demerits of any kind of religious approach to solving economic questions. The Christian approach is then more toward depth and stresses the eternal unchanging *now* of God's presence, yet in such Gospel sections as the Beatitudes or the admonitions concerning charity to others in the Last Judgment narratives, it is also aware of the complexities of the surface factors. Judaism, on the other hand, is more sharply aware of these multidimensional surface factors, but in the searing insights of the Prophets and other writers it is also aware of the unchanging, eternal dimensions.

Might we not forge a revitalized economic mythology of Judeo-Christianity which, blending both factors, allows us to embrace with joy the complexity of worldwide problems, but allows us also to anchor these problems in a deeper unchanging reality which tells us constantly that, important as they are, they are not the ultimate concerns of our life? The conjunction of the two factors might afford a strong and balanced view of life and economics and keep us from oversimplification.

MINISESSION A

Dr. Joseph C. Finney: We have two distinguished speakers today, Professor Mary McDermott of nursing and Professor Jan Savitz of biology. The paper was jointly prepared. The first part will be presented by Professor McDermott; the second by Professor Savitz.

Cheating: What Are Your Responsibilities?

Dr. Mary Ann McDermott
Dr. Jan Savitz

For at least several decades, this university has been plagued with a particular form of injustice within its classroom walls—dishonesty. Excessive competition, and faculty and administrative laxity resulting in examination theft and widespread cheating, especially among the pre-health-profession students, were reported last spring. An investigating committee was appointed, charges were made, sanctions were issued, a hearing board reviewed disputed charges or sanctions, and appeals were made to the vice-president. At least one of these cases is still in process and has gained local media attention.

This type of injustice in the classroom is not new or unique to Loyola; however, considerable attention was awarded to it because of the large number of students, departments, and courses involved. The accounts are similar to those reported at the University of Maryland last year and in the United States military academies four years ago. All reports seem to bear out the findings reported by Parr in the 1930s and by Bowers in the 1960s that 40-60 percent of college students, on self-report, admit to involvement in some form of academic dishonesty.[1] In both studies cheating was defined in a conservative way, and Bower pointed out that there was reason to believe that cheating was more prevalent among those failing to return the survey instrument than among those participating in the sample.[2]

The situation last spring also merited attention because the students involved could be generally characterized as academically able. This observation was in contrast to the data gathered by Bowers that demonstrated that the "poorest students are the ones most likely to cheat . . . those who take their role as student most lightly, those who study neither long nor efficiently."[3] Bowers concluded that "presumably students who place primary emphasis on intellectual matters are more committed to the academic life and more sensitive to the norms of academic integrity that govern it."[4] Quite noticeably our integrity had been wounded and our trust in those most expected to honor that commitment had been misplaced. We have been hurt where we are most vulnerable, through an attack on a value we hold most dear, by a group we expect to cherish that value as we do.

Administrators and faculty have offered a number of reasons why cheating occurred. Pressure always enters into the discussion. A recent study conducted in an eastern public university asked undergraduate students why they thought their fellow college students cheated. Three of the five top reasons given were clearly related to the pressure factor: better grades, 94.7 percent; too much pressure to complete work on time, 75.6 percent; demand for scholastic distinction, 72.5 percent. However, two of the five motives, in the opinions of the surveyed students, were in no way related to pressure.

Students suggested that the ease with which one can cheat in the classroom encourages dishonesty. Eighty percent said that they think students cheat because it is very easy to do so in some courses; 69.5 percent blamed cheating on the fact that some teachers do not enforce the honor system.[5]

The study showed that parental pressure to achieve was not a great factor among the reasons for cheating. We would comment that the literature and the nature of our student body lead us to believe that this might be a stronger factor in our institution than was found in that study. Overall, however, we believe that these reasons for cheating do indeed reflect our own academic setting.

We recognize that the pressure factor—for grades, for completing the amount of work required in a given amount of time, for academic distinction, for places in professional and graduate school, for success—is probably never going to ease. It will be the task of the remainder of this paper to examine the inherent responsibilities of those in the academic environment who are charged with facilitating justice in the classroom, to lessen the ease with which one can cheat. We do not do this in an accusatory manner, although certain aspects may take on that flavor, and we admit that blaming ourselves, our colleagues, and our students did cross our minds, as we proceeded to develop this paper. We have decided to go, however, with "job descriptions" for those administrators, faculty, and students (individually and collectively) in the Loyola community who are desirous of facilitating an environment for academic honesty.

Administrator Responsibilities

Administrators are often perceived by others in the academic community, and sometimes even view themselves, as being far removed from what goes on in the day-to-day sanctity of the classroom. Nothing could be further from the truth, especially where justice and honesty are concerned. Twelve specific areas where administrators need to exert leadership in facilitating justice in the classroom come to mind.

1. Adequate support in providing human resources, such as secretaries, laboratory assistants, proctors, and computer center staff. This would eliminate the need for student workers in typing, handling, or grading exams.

   Example: Biology Department

   a) There was one full-time secretary for 16 faculty and there were at least 1,100 majors in biology, plus 200 nursing students. Some students were involved in duplicating and collating exams and quizzes. Although none of these student helpers were involved in cheating, the potential for cheating existed.

   b) There are several biology classes taught each semester that have between 100 and 300 students enrolled. Since these are laboratory courses (four hours of lab each week) this means that there are four to twelve laboratory sections for each of these courses. A large percentage of these laboratories are taught by undergraduates who have received good grades in the course. In some instances these students make up the quizzes for their laboratories. This is potentially a bad situation, since some portion of the final grade is in the hands of undergraduates; furthermore the students could receive inadequate instruction in the laboratory.

   c) Proctors are usually undergraduates.

   d) Some students working on grading exams at the computer center last year bragged about their ability to change grades for other students. I suspect this is possible, and some students believe this occurs.

2. Awareness of the need for careful handling of official documents, particularly change-of-grade forms.

3. Adequate compensation for faculty. If faculty feels short-changed or cheated, with regard to salaries or support from the administration, they may tend to overlook students'

cheating. "Why should I bother?" How important this attitude is is unknown. With certain faculty it may be a key factor.

4. Administrative support when faculty enforce honesty in the classroom:

    a) availability to discuss specific instances of classroom injustice;

    b) information regarding legal counsel, which I understand will be given to our faculty in the near future;

    c) sympathetic listening and good counsel.

    Faculty fear litigation from student offenders. It is a very chilling experience. Nontenured faculty may be reluctant to enter disputes on student cheating. They may become well known in a negative sense by the administration because, whether the faculty member is right or wrong in the particular case, he or she becomes the center of controversy. While faculty should expect the administration to be objective, they should also feel that they have the support of the administration, and that the administration is dealing openly with them.

5. Administrators must facilitate the development and implementation of academic and disciplinary grievance procedures. The faculty should be aware of the grievance procedures at the departmental, college and vice-president, and dean of faculties levels.

6. Students should be aware of grievance procedures and the proper chain of command regarding classroom grievances, whether they be capricious grading systems, observations of cheating, or class mismanagement. Most students are uninformed about, or at least inexperienced in relating to the educational hierarchy. Has the Board of Undergraduate Studies statement on academic dishonesty been circulated in any systematic manner to the student body? Are students aware that the dean's office has on file the grievance procedure for each department?

7. Adequate classroom space must be a high priority in the planning by administration. Students are herded into large lecture halls in a standing-room-only situation that makes the fire marshal cringe; it is just possible that students may feel little respect for the individual worth and dignity we espouse in our mission statement. The temptation to look

at another's exam paper, pass notes, come to the examination with ponies or a crib sheet is easy to yield to when the faculty member does not even know the student's name, or does not really care if the student is present. "The class is just too large to bother with taking roll." Students may at least in part view their dishonesty as acts directed against what they perceive as the big, cold, impersonal, Loyola system.

8. Related to the problem of adequate space is the planning of schedules with a concern for the dimension of time. We recognize that there are prime-time problems; however, the space-scheduling problems prevent many students from seeking gainful employment or becoming involved on any regular basis in cocurricular activities. A student could at least in theory have classes and labs in the sciences from 8:30 A.M. to 10:30 P.M. several days a week. When students feel cheated, the temptation to reciprocate is increased.

9. Faculty development programs concerning dishonesty, cheating, plagiarism, and theft are needed. These are topics seldom discussed in a scholarly manner in the literature and even less as program content in faculty in-service programs. Bitching and gossip among faculty, however, testify to faculty interest in the topic. Faculty need to be assisted in developing knowledge, attitudes, and skills to prevent, observe, and handle these classroom injustices. If the older statistics are to be believed, brighter students did not cheat as much as their less highly motivated peers. Thus some of the present faculty, educated in the 1940s and 1950s, are relatively ignorant regarding cheating from a personal experiential data base.

10. Administrators should remind themselves that there is no honor system operant at Loyola. Primary preventive measures should be initiated by administrators from the top down to enforce the existent academic honesty policy. The vagueness or cumbersomeness of the present policies must be eliminated. Hopefully this will encourage faculty to report cases of academic dishonesty to the chairman's and the dean's offices. A cumulative record of dishonesty should give cause for consideration by the department chairman or dean to recommend suspension or separation from the university.

11. Administrators, i.e., department chairmen and deans, in conjunction with faculty, need to insure that appropriate and legitimate sanctions be issued. What are the penalty options? Is the lowering of a letter grade or the issuing of an *F* for a particular test an appropriate sanction for cheating on that test? Can the faculty legitimately lower an individual's course grade one letter, or issue a course grade of *F,* for cheating on a single test? Recognizing that the rationale for the issuing of the failing grade never is exhibited on a student's transcript, is the penalty severe enough in all cases? Should recommendations to professional and graduate schools contain this information? What penalty is appropriate and legitimate for students not presently enrolled in a course who are involved in the theft or sale and distribution of course examination materials? How is the student who cheats in several courses at concurrent or different times in his college career ever identified? Are faculty obliged to notify their chairman or dean of each instance of cheating, or does the chairman or dean only need to be informed if and when the student requests a grievance proceeding? What constitutes an act serious enough to consider probation or separation—or what accumulation of *venials* makes up a *mortal*? When penalties imposed by faculty, department, or dean are appealed by the student, should there be any recourse for the faculty, department chairman, or dean who does not feel that justice for all has been served?

12. The last point is also one that is applicable to faculty. It may seem out of place in this discussion; however, it is a sore point on this campus at this time. Faculty and administrators expect students to be ethical. When students are reported to revel in their dishonest acts, celebrate to rejoice in the possession of a stolen exam, refuse to be remorseful when confronted with evidence of a dishonest act, we are understandably irate. Consequently the outraged faculty and administration have the temptation to conduct themselves in their handling of the students less than admirably. In our everyday affairs we speak about others as zealous or as vigilant; the characteristics have a favorable connotation. However, when we refer to a zealot or to a vigilante, the connotation changes markedly. Zealous and vigilant faculty

and administrators in their condemnation of cheating must watch carefully so as not to take on the characteristics of the zealot or the vigilante in their pursuit of cheaters. Justice in these instances is rarely tempered by mercy—truly a sad state of affairs. This has implications for the entire academic community in terms of faculty-student relationships. Students hopefully will be more inclined to be moved towards remorse if confronted with their guilt rather than with uncontrolled anger. Just anger is certainly understandable, but we must remember we are making judgments about specific acts of behavior, not of personalities. When going after the offenders, is there the possibility of exercising such a characteristic as relaxed vigilance—relaxed in the sense that it is not tainted by vengeance, spite, vindictiveness?

Faculty Responsibilities

Faculty need to dare to demand honesty. Moral condemnation and administrative policies are not viewed as sufficient responses to the incidents of cheating that we and others are encountering. The expectation of honesty in terms of justice needs to be shared with students in every course in the university at the beginning of each semester, orally and in writing. The expectation should be reinforced often during the semester. It is presumed that the foremost constraint against cheating is a student's own moral stance on cheating—his feeling that cheating is wrong.[6] The faculty need to affirm that moral stance.

In terms of justice the faculty also need to demand honesty of themselves in their relationships with students. Honesty and justice seem to be reciprocated by individuals experiencing these values. This requirement demands a considerable output of time and energy in the following course preparation and implementation activities.

1. The syllabi for the course should provide course expectations, evaluative methods, and the grading system. The oral introduction to a syllabus might include our suggestions as to how to study for this course, our expectations as to a time commitment to study, the availability of tutoring, and certainly a reference to our being accessible for discussion of students' course-related problems.

2. The expectation of student success needs to be communicated by the faculty member to the students early; however, success need not be operationally defined as achieving an *A* in the course. The admission policy of this university on the whole implies that the expectation of success is a reasonable one for most students in most courses, granted the students' motivation, adequate time, and the necessary background of prerequisites. Faculty need to remind students who fail or achieve lower grades than expected that the cause was possibly the students' inability to demonstrate mastery, or lack of motivation, time, or prerequisites. Students who do not attend class regularly or are consistently late, are involved in taking prerequisites concurrently, are taking an overload, or do not take the time to meet with the faculty member for help at scheduled office hours need to be admonished for their behavior. This presupposes that the faculty member takes roll, values promptness, has published office hours, and is conscientious in his own academic advising regarding concurrent prerequisites and in permitting academic overloads. The element of trust and genuine concern, essential to all successful relationships, is communicated well when these conditions are met. If you do your part, I'll do mine. Success, at least at the mastery level, can be achieved.

3. Assignments need to be appropriate in content, length, and pacing during the semester. Students often become extremely anxious. Assignments do not seem relevant to their learning. There are too many pages to read or write. Books for required library assignments often turn out to be inaccessible. Papers are due in all five courses during the same week of the semester. Cross-department planning is not feasible, but letting students know far enough in advance when assignments are due at least assists their planning.

4. Faculty should share the *how, when,* and *what* of testing with their students. To study well for a test the student really does need to know its general structure, whether objective or essay, and its approximate length. Knowing the dates for tests well in advance gives the student a work plan for the semester. That pop quizzes are to be expected in a particular course should be made clear from the start. The *what* to be tested may be as precise as a list of specific learner-oriented content objectives or as general as a statement like "You are expected to read

the text; however, the test questions will be drawn primarily from my lectures."

5. Dr. Savitz will be moving into the structuring of an environment to facilitate honesty and justice during the evaluation stage of the teaching-learning process, that point at which the possibility of deception is most likely to occur; however, it is our own personal experience that many of us don't like to consider ourselves watchdogs. That's not why we became teachers. We feel that students treated with honesty will always reciprocate. Can you remember the first time you realized students in your classroom cheated? You always knew they did in Dr. So-and-So's class, but he was such a . . . he deserved it. But I teach well and treat students with respect. I implore each of you to be honest, set aside naivete, and engage fully in the next activity.

6. Setting up the environment to facilitate honesty and justice during the examinations involves not only an attitude toward testing but also the mechanics of testing. To facilitate their assessment of these concerns, an examination of conscience for faculty is presented here.

An Examination of Conscience on Testing

Attitude
1. What is the purpose of testing, and is there more than one purpose?
2. Do I rewrite exams every time I teach a course?
   a) Do I obtain questions from students' guides?
   b) If I don't think of new questions, why should students have new answers?
3. What are the advantages and disadvantages of having a test pool of questions (which students may see) from which examinations will be taken?
4. Do I ask questions that allow the student to apply his knowledge rather than demonstrate his ability to memorize by rote?
5. Do I return exams so that students may learn from their mistakes?
6. Do my exams test concepts and facts that I have emphasized?
7. Do I determine grades justly?

8. Do I insure the security of my grade book or keep records till one year after the grade has been given?
9. Do I have procedures to apply so that suspected cheating does not continue through a given examination?
10. Have I developed methods to reduce or eliminate cheating on future examinations?
11. What evidence do I gather to demonstrate dishonest behavior rather than relying on suspicion or hearsay?
12. Do I know the proper means for bringing a dishonest student to justice within the system?
13. Have I clarified my own values in regard to the long- and short-term consequences of student dishonesty, to the student's present and future career, to his peers, and to the faculty?

Mechanics
1. Who types my exams? Is it a staff person or myself?
2. Is the exam stored in a secure place until time for the test?
3. Is each test prepared in two or more forms or otherwise designed to prevent cheating?
4. Is the size of the test room sufficient to insure adequate spacing of students?
5. Is there sufficient time for the examination? Should I give more time or a shorter test?
6. Can all students be tested at the same time or during the same day to lower the incidence of disclosure of exam questions?
7. Are the students who take the exam the students enrolled in the course?
8. Do I have knowledgeable and trustworthy proctors who take their job seriously?

Student Responsibilities

The responsibilities of students will seem to be brief and perhaps broader than those listed for faculty and administrators. We will focus on two major responsibilities of students.

1. Students should not cheat, because their own self-respect and personal integrity are jeopardized by cheating. One would expect that these personal attributes should be important to everyone. Cheating also creates a climate of mistrust, defeatism, and a negative attitude toward real learning.

2. Open communication between faculty and students is a shared responsibility. If the expectations of trust, concern, and success have been communicated by faculty, and a demonstration of accessibility and availability has been made, much will already have occurred to insure honesty and justice in the classroom. The university's contract with the student implies an expectation that both faculty and students have a similar intention to pursue truth with honesty and forthrightness. Students need to know that, should this ideal environment be jeopardized, it is then their responsibility individually or collectively to communicate this breach of contract to the teacher: "The test is out; there is cheating." Students need to share information of both generalities and specifics and to be assured that their anonymity will be guaranteed. However, students must also consider the possibility, should the matter go still further, of the need to risk their anonymity in the name of justice.

3. We stated earlier that the foremost constraint against cheating is a student's own moral stance on cheating, and we attempted to identify ways in which the faculty can affirm that moral stance. Another important constraining force is the feeling of disapproval among the student's peers. Ideas and feelings about cheating are highly influenced by the peer group. Students who truly are interested in promoting justice in the academic environment will not only *not* cheat themselves and will report occurrences of cheating to those in charge, but also will seek to limit cheating, at least among those students they know, by expressing their personal feelings about it to roommates, lab partners, those in their fraternities and sororities, those on their teams, in the school newspaper. They will encourage those peers to take a responsible attitude toward cheating. Evidence indicates that their influence will be felt. To bring the full impact of peer disapproval to bear at Loyola, a large-scale student effort is essential. Although we are not recommending an honor system at Loyola at this time, it is interesting to note that, in the Bowers study,

The level of cheating is much lower at schools that place primary responsibility for dealing with cases of academic dishonesty in the hands of the students and their elected representatives, as under the honor system, than at schools that rely on faculty-centered control or have a form of mixed control. . . . Presumably, in return for the privileges and trust students are accorded under the honor system, they develop a stronger sense of commitment to norms of academic integrity and, thereby, a strong climate of peer disapproval of cheating emerges on the campus.[7]

In summary, justice is compromised in an academic environment where cheating is prevalent. Cheating creates a demoralizing environment in which the pursuit of intellectual goals is frustrated for all. An expenditure of time and energy by the department chairmen or deans is involved in following up on cases, reviewing records of implicated students, consulting with faculty, appointing grievance committees, testifying before hearing boards—time that might be better spent on activities more central to the academic mission of the university. Faculty are frustrated in their efforts to engender a love for learning and are transformed instead into watchdogs, always on the lookout for cheating in their correction of assignments or administration of a test. Serious, honest students are cheated of an appropriate setting for stimulating intellectual growth and academic integrity.

By taking seriously the responsibilities we have outlined in this paper, hopefully the entire academic community—administrators, faculty, and students alike—can take steps to restore an academic setting that embraces honesty in its classrooms. Dare to demand it!

Notes

1. F. W. Parr, as cited in William J. Bowers, *Student Dishonesty and Its Control in College* (New York: Columbia University, Bureau of Applied Social Research, 1964), pp. 193-194.

2. Bowers, *Student Dishonesty,* pp. 193-194.

3. Ibid., pp. 82-83.

4. Ibid., p. 195.

5. Betty Lou Raskin, "Cheating Is Easier Than Studying," *National Newsletter of Pi Lambda Theta,* vol. 25, No. 1 (Sept.-Oct. 1980), p. 4.

6. William J. Bowers, "Confronting College Cheating," in *Campus Values,* ed. Charles W. Havice (New York: Charles Scribner's Sons, 1968), p. 79.

7. Bowers, *Student Dishonesty,* p. 198.

MINISESSION B

Dr. Edward M. Levine: I would like to introduce to you Father Joseph H. Boel, S.J., a member of the university ministry at Loyola. A native of Belgium, Father Boel entered the Society of Jesus in 1946. He did his seminary preparation in Belgium and in India, where he was ordained in 1959. He has also studied sociology in India and at the University of Amsterdam in the Netherlands. He taught sociology at St. Xavier College in India and was a staff member of the Indian Social Institute in Delhi. He spent three years in Pakistan as a member of Loyola Hall, which is an institute for dialogue between Muslims and Christians.

Without further ado, let me present to you Father Boel.

Five Barley Loaves and Two Fishes:
Education for Faith and Justice
Father Joseph H. Boel, S.J.

"How do we educate for faith and justice, in the face of declining world resources, increasing unemployment, increasing population, in the face of professional pressures, in the face of technological societies?" I want to focus on certain aspects of this question and reflect on what education for faith and justice could mean in a world facing increasing scarcity of resources and rising expectations among a growing world population.

I want to avoid a possible misunderstanding. I do not consider education for faith and justice something totally new, as if the educational process would ever have been defined in terms of education for unbelief and injustice. If, however, faith and justice have to be considered objectives that deserve special emphasis in the process of learning, it is for the simple reason that they are related to a future of our world and of our society, which for many has become doubtful and uncertain. We are constantly besieged by events, facts, and figures that impede belief in a future where justice prevails. One senses in our culture a "pervasive despair of understanding the course of modern history or of subjecting it to rational direction."[1] Our age has been compared to that of *fin de siècle* Vienna with its "national paralysis in the face of serious economic, social, and institutional challenges."[2] Some have suggested a course on the history of the future, dealing with such questions as: "What images of the future does our society possess? Where will we get our food, and how can it be appropriately distributed? What about our energy supply, and how can it be equitably shared? How can we reduce the poisons in the atmosphere? Can we have a proper balance between population and the life-support systems of this planet? How can we live together, with civility, in a climate of constraint?"[3] Father Peter Henriot, S.J., of the Center of Concern in Washington, D.C., speaking at Seattle University, made his audience slightly uneasy when he urged them to ask themselves whether their education was relevant to the year 2000 in the light of inescapable global problems. He also expressed the hope "that the motto around Seattle University was not: 'We'll make it through more of the same,' but rather 'Let's dare to change, try something different.'"

In this context of uncertainty and doubt, the question regarding education for faith and justice must be raised. Faith is used here to mean faith in the future, faith in our capacity to give direction to the course of events, and not only religious belief, though this is certainly part of the general notion of faith, as will be explained later. Again when I speak of education I do not simply refer to education in the classroom. Faith and justice form part of the human experience, which does not distinguish between teacher and student. This however does not mean that, in the course of this discussion, something like a broad outline of a course on faith and justice may not emerge.

Education for faith and justice, as I shall develop in this paper, consists first in a confrontation with the situation as it exists today. This is to be followed by an examination of the various interpretations that can be given to these facts, so as to be able to arrive at a choice from among various alternative views. It will be a choice not so much between faith and unbelief, justice and injustice, as between various modalities of believing and various ways of implementing justice. Third, this cognitive aspect of the educational process must be complemented by the creation of what Kohlberg calls an environment, a moral atmosphere, and we shall have to look at what this means in the context of a university institution. Finally I hope by the end of this paper to have shown that education for faith and justice is to be considered an essential part of the education of the total person. If I succeed, then the enigmatic title of this paper may go a long way to explain it all.

Education of the Eyes

Education for faith and justice consists first in what Teilhard de Chardin, in a different but not totally unrelated context, calls "the education of the eyes." This idea is not as easy as it may appear to be. We are constantly flooded with facts and figures, and overwhelmed by a spate of events which more often than not serve as a smokescreen, making it difficult to discern what to believe and how to act. We are easily affected by what Barbara Ward calls the "tunnel vision" of most "developed peoples."

> Although they make up no more than a third of the human race, they find it exceptionally difficult to focus their minds on the two-thirds of humanity with whom they share the biosphere. Like elephants round the water hole, they not only do not notice the other thirsty animals. It hardly crosses their minds that they may be trampling the place to ruin.[4]

What I mean by the factual situation may be illustrated by referring to a major issue which our world is facing today. The world population increased from one billion in 1820 to four billion in 1976. It is estimated that if the present rate of growth continues, by the first decade of the next century, "a whole new world, equivalent in numbers to this one, will be piled on top of the present level of population."[5] Whereas by the end of the last century 15 percent of the world population lived in urban centers of more than 20,000 inhabitants, by the end of this century there will be more urban dwellers than rural people, i.e., a total of three and one half billion, which represents the total world population of 1965. There will be 273 one-million cities by 1985, 147 of them in developing countries. In 1950, there were two ten-million cities: New York and London. By 1985, their numbers will have increased to seventeen, of which more than half will be in developing areas.

This population increase is not simply a matter of statistical exercise. It occurs in the context of rising expectations on the part of people wanting to live, like everyone else, a decent human life. They all share in "the deepening conquest of the human indignation by a dimly perceived but passionately longed-for vision of equality and dignity for every human being." Their cry "for greater justice and dignity . . . will not be stilled. On the contrary, it will be raised all the more insistently as numbers and pressures increase."[6]

This cry must be placed in an ecological context of diminishing resources and the general deterioration of the environment. The creation of even the "minimum physical conditions of a worthy human existence" will constitute a "tremendous physical task" and will raise wholly new questions about the use and abuse of the necessary resources. It will also demand "little short of a new agricultural revolution."[7]

These have to be confronted before we can ask ourselves questions regarding faith and justice, which after all have to be lived and acted upon in this world.

Interpretation of the Facts

Facts, however, do not speak by themselves. What is more difficult and also more important is the way we analyze them and understand their implications. An acquaintance with the various controversial views as regards the ethical implications of the factual data is a necessary step in the education for faith and justice.

First, it may be good to ask ourselves whether we feel it necessary to view these issues with any degree of seriousness and concern. The compelling nature of our immediate concerns often makes it difficult to focus our attention on issues pertaining to the future. We tend to treat with benign neglect those reports that "dare suggest nations shape their policies according to global cooperation, not mutual suspicion."[8] When Ronald Reagan was asked how he proposed to respond to the long-term implications of overpopulation, resource depletion, and degradation of the environment, he said that he was not particularly concerned and that he "didn't see much accuracy in past reports on future problems." Yet he spoke approvingly of studies saying that "the earth can support a population of twenty-eight billion people." Comments McCarthy: "Perhaps so, if a planetary Calcutta can be imagined. What it can't support is a population that has no leaders daring enough to think beyond tomorrow."[9]

Let us not too easily blame our leaders. I mention this example because it reveals an attitude which is perhaps more widespread than we care to admit. We all too easily tend to look

away from what we prefer to ignore and to believe that somehow we'll find a way out without too much trying.

Between Hope and Despair

Once we allow ourselves to be confronted with the facts, the
question arises whether and how we can come to an understanding of what they have to tell us. The message is by no means
clear. There are quite a few who, in their search for a meaningful interpretation of the factual situation, oscillate between
hope and despair; for it is realized that the outcome can by no
means be seen as a guaranteed success. A typical exemplar of
this uncertainty is Robert Heilbroner, a philosopher and economist. In the introduction to *An Enquiry into the Human Prospect* he warns that: "The outlook for man . . . is painful, difficult,
perhaps desperate," and that he can hardly conceive of the future other than "as a continuation of the darkness, cruelty, and
disorder of the past."[10] He comes to the conclusion that we
must brace ourselves for "wars of redistribution of wealth as
poor nations try to capture a larger share in the ever diminishing
available resources and products. If by the question, 'Is there
hope for man?' we ask whether it is possible to meet the challenges of the future without the payment of a fearful price, the
answer must be: 'No, there is no such hope.'"[11]

This is a significant departure from what Heilbroner wrote in
an earlier work, *The Future as History,* in which he expressed
the belief that the forces of history still "point in the direction
of optimism and progress."[12] In the latest edition of his book,
The Worldly Philosophers, he seems to return to a guarded
optimism.

> After two centuries of sailing mainly as the winds directed us, the
> tiller of society is again in our grasp. More and more we have taken on
> our own shoulders the responsibility for selecting our destination—
> with all the inescapable dangers as well as the chances for progress that
> active navigation must bring.[13]

The faint hope emerges that our destiny is in our hands provided we are willing to adopt an imaginative approach to the
direction of our society. Even in a free society, we must not allow economic forces to determine the course of history. More
and more we are interfering with what used to be considered as
an autonomous process of development. Active interference,

however, can again be understood in various different ways, each providing a different interpretation of what is meant by our responsibility for selecting a blueprint for the world's future.

Ethics of Despair

According to Garrett Hardin's "lifeboat ethics," the richer nations must make a decision: either try to save the poor of the world and, given the limited resources at our disposal, go down along with them, or allow nature to take its course, as long as there is no way to impose population controls that would reduce the number of hungry mouths to be fed.

A similar position is held by those who advocate what has become known as the application of a system of triage to the food policy. This would consist in giving assistance only to those who deserve it and who are likely to be helped by it.

> Only one nation, the United States, has a sizable surplus of food. And, with godlike finality, we dispense it, after systematically deciding which people are salvageable and should be fed, which will survive without help, and which are hopeless and should be left to the ravages of famine.[14]

It would be too simplistic to ignore these approaches to policymaking, since they express ideas and voice fears and apprehensions which are by no means confined to scholarly articles and books. They are rooted in a sense of hopelessness regarding issues that seem to be beyond our control. They challenge us to reflect on our own convictions and attitudes and force us to examine our own beliefs regarding the future and the possibility of bringing about a world where justice prevails.

Ethics of Hope

The positions outlined in the previous section rest on the assumption that if we are to find a solution to our problems, we must be willing to impose certain demands on those who are now dependent on the aid of developed countries. It is they who, for example, must reduce their population growth and who must adopt institutional changes for our aid to be effective. Our own institutional arrangements and way of life are largely ignored.

This is not the only option available to us. Others continue to believe in another kind of future and in the implementation of a kind of justice rooted in values and principles that are part of our Judeo-Christian tradition. Their search for a viable world order based on this tradition leads them to look at our own patterns of production and consumption, which have come to be taken for granted. In this critical analysis they find a new source of hope for the future. Barbara Ward writes:

> In short, no problem is insoluble in the creation of a balanced and conserving planet save humanity itself. Can it reach in time the vision of joint survival? Can its inescapable physical interdependence—the chief new insight of our century—induce that vision? We do not know. We have the duty to hope.[15]

Ward reaches this conclusion after having dealt with the problems of nuclear energy, unemployment, and development assistance. Her basic approach consists in demonstrating "by working examples of how changes—even very great changes—can be brought about."[16] These changes do not simply apply to the poorer nations, but to our own living arrangements, our methods of production, and the application of technological know-how.

As regards energy resources, for example, we take for granted that energy consumption must rise in order to maintain economic growth. This assumption however is no longer true for most Western nations.

> Indeed, the nations with the highest per capita energy consumption could over the next few decades reduce their fuel consumption while actually improving living standards and achieving genuine economic growth.[17]

An important aspect of the energy problem is the development of alternative energy resources. Yet, as is the case in most Western nations, only 3.7 percent of the budget of the United States Department of Energy has been allocated for research in renewable energy resources since 1978;[18] yet report after report has been issued with the urgent warning: "All sectors of our nation's economy must begin immediately to significantly reduce the demand for nonrenewable energy resources such as oil and natural gas."[19] Similar examples in the realm of conservation of energy could have a considerable impact on the level of unemployment.[20]

Equally relevant to this discussion is the kind of critical analysis to be found in Michael Harrington's *Decade of Decision.* He analyzes domestic problems in terms of a "crisis of the system" of our society and advocates changes in the direction of wider participation of the people in the economic process and of true democratization. We may not like this approach; yet it would be unwise to dismiss offhand the voices calling for "democratic alternatives to corporate domination" when it is realized, for example, that "since 1973 every major photovoltaic firm has been acquired by the oil industry,"[21] and that by the end of this decade world production of industrial goods will be largely concentrated in the hands of 300 giant firms, of which 200 will be American.[22] A social and political framework must be found to subordinate corporate power to the wider interests of society.

I have tried in this second part to summarize some of the various interpretations that can be given of our present situation. It should be clear by now that we need to search for a definition of social justice that can provide the philosophical foundation for a sense of responsibility for a common future. The works of John Rawls and Peter Singer are particularly relevant. We shall then have to see how we can arrive at an understanding of how we can live a life of faith in the God of history, and how in the light of that faith we can find a meaningful approach to the promotion of justice. Here I find particularly helpful Avery Dulles's study on "The Meaning of Faith Considered in Relationship to Justice."[23]

Defining Social Justice

I wish to illustrate how attempts are being made to come to an understanding of social justice on philosophical grounds. Rawls, for example, presents as the basis of a just society the "difference principle," which he defines as follows:

> All social primary goods—liberty and opportunity, income and wealth, and the bases of self-respect—are to be distributed equally unless an unequal distribution of any or all of these goods is to the advantage of the least favored.[24]

This means that higher rewards can be given to certain groups of our society if giving them improves the lot of the least advantaged groups who would then profit from the added economic activity made possible by those who are economically in a more advantageous position.

Peter Singer, on the other hand, takes as his starting point the way people reacted to the situation in Bengal in 1971, and he argues that it cannot be justified: "Indeed the whole way we look at moral issues—our moral conceptual scheme—needs to be altered, and with it the way of life that has come to be taken for granted in our society."[25] The outcome of his argument is "that our traditional moral categories are upset. The traditional distinction between duty and charity cannot be drawn, or at least, not in the place we normally draw it."[26]

An acquaintance with these attempts should form an integral part of the education for faith and justice. For ideas continue to be important. And yet can they provide the necessary vision and motivation that enable us to overcome the forces that pull us away from implementing what we believe to be right, and to do so also when the final result of our striving remains in doubt?

Faith That Does Justice

It is at this point that the religious dimension of faith must be examined, not as something added to all the rest, but as providing an encompassing vision and a motivational factor that speak to the total person. Education of the eyes then becomes an education of the eyes of faith, a conversion of the heart, enabling us to see in the "dimly perceived but passionately longed-for vision of equality and dignity for every human being"[27] the vision of the prophets and saints calling the believer to "undo the yoke, to let the enslaved go free . . . sharing your bread with the hungry and bringing the homeless into your house." (Is. 58:6-7)

From the study of Avery Dulles I would like to cite two points that I find especially relevant to this discussion. First, besides the "intellectualist" and the "fiducial" approach to faith, we can look at faith from a "performative" point of view and define it in terms of "a combination of commitment and discernment" which must be seen as being "inseparably united aspects of the disclosure experience, so that the illumination of faith is given only within a commitment to appropriate action."[28] In this perspective we can understand the meaning of the words of Jesus: "Whatever you have done to the least of these, you have done to me." In the process of reaching out to the need of the other, to "the cry of the poor," one comes to know and understand who Christ is, what Christ is all about: a disclosure experience in the very act of commitment.

The second point is related to the biblical meaning of the kingdom of God which, though never fully realized in historical time, yet must be considered as "a reality at work within history."[29] It is a reality that "stimulates our creative imagination so that we find ever new ways of provisionally realizing within history signs and anticipations of the promised Kingdom."[30]

> ... through faith we become instruments in the healing and reconciliation of the broken world. We become agents of justice and bearers of the power of the Kingdom. Faith, therefore, is more than intellectual assent, more than hope in what God will do without us; it is also a present participation in the work that God is doing—that is to say, in the task of bringing forth justice to nations.[31]

In this perspective, living a life of faith and commitment to the promotion of justice becomes part of the reality of faith that *does* justice. This brings us to the consideration of an aspect of education which emphasizes what Kohlberg calls "social" rather than "cognitive" stimulation and which consists in social interaction, moral dialogue, and moral decision-making in the context of a moral atmosphere or the "justice structure" of an institution.[32]

Experiential Aspect of Education for Faith and Justice

Education for faith and justice can take place only in an environment where justice forms part of a person's experience and where opportunities are provided to take an active part in the promotion of justice. Being exposed to a just institutional structure and to persons who do justice is as important as being taught about faith and justice. Is it sufficient, however, for a university like Loyola to think only in terms of the creation of a general institutional environment? Has it not become necessary for the university to give a more visible expression to its commitment to faith and justice? This symposium and the course on world hunger and on environmental problems are steps in this direction, but are they enough?

Again, haven't we to reconsider the place of those activities which are now considered to be extracurricular but which, in fact, create possibilities for personal involvement in issues related to social justice? Many examples could be mentioned—Amnesty International, the Hunger Week, Pax Christi, the group working among Cambodian refugees, among the poor of the neighborhood. Are they not to be considered as an integral part of the educational process? It would then be possible to emphasize, in the context of these activities, an ongoing process of reflection on the issues. This would also facilitate a growing awareness that, however complex and intractable the issues may seem to be, there remains the duty to hope and to believe that each person is part of the solution and that this solution has to start in the *here* and *now* of one's own personal situation.

Conclusion

Finally the title of this paper still remains to be explained. It is taken from the gospel according to John, chapter six, which contains the story of the multiplication of the bread. There was a crowd of 5,000 men, not to mention the women and children. The apostles suggested to Jesus that the crowd be sent away, for the place was isolated and there was no way to find food for all the people. One of the apostles mentioned in passing that there was a boy there who had five barley loaves and two fishes. Now I cannot imagine this boy being noticed in such a large crowd, if the boy himself had not somehow made his presence known. He must have made his way through the crowd, to the place where the action took place and where he was able to hear Jesus and his men talking among themselves. When he heard what they were talking about, he must have come forward with his loaves and fishes.

The reaction of the apostles was predictable. But Jesus took the loaves and the fishes and blessed them. The hungry crowd was fed and received nourishment in abundance.

Education for faith and justice consists, in the first place, in making ourselves and others aware of the world that is in the making. Looking at this complex world, we are faced with a choice regarding the way we conceive of its future. And it is to be hoped that the choice we make is based on the conviction that in the midst of uncertainty and doubt we can still hope for a future world where justice prevails, provided we are willing to contribute whatever we have and whatever we are. This contribution may very well seem to be nothing but a couple of loaves and some fish. But then, who is there to say that miracles, big or small, are no longer part of the real world?

Notes

1. Christopher Lasch, *The Culture of Narcissism* (New York: W. W. Norton & Co., 1979), p. 18.

2. L. Botstein, "The Vienna Analogy," *The New Republic,* 20 December 1980, p. 27.

3. E. L. Boyer, "The College Curriculum: Our Search for Common Ground," *Chicago Tribune,* 23 November 1978, p. 10.

4. Barbara Ward and Rene Dubos, *Only One Earth* (New York: W. W. Norton & Co., 1972), p. 145.

5. Ibid., p. 2.

6. Barbara Ward, *The Home of Man* (New York: W. W. Norton & Co., 1967), p. 5.

7. Ibid., p. 7.

8. C. McCarthy, "A Future Already Forgotten," *Chicago Tribune,* 24 February 1981, section 2, p. 3.

9. Ibid.

10. Robert Heilbroner, *An Enquiry into the Human Prospect* (New York: W. W. Norton & Co., 1974), p. 22.

11. Ibid., pp. 136-137.

12. *The Future as History* (New York: Harper & Row, 1959), p. 209.

13. *The Worldly Philosophers,* 5th ed. (New York: Simon & Schuster, 1980), p. 318.

14. W. Greene, "Triage," *New York Times Magazine,* 5 January 1975, p. 9.

15. Barbara Ward, *Progress for a Small Planet* (New York: W. W. Norton & Co., 1979), p. 277.

16. Ibid., p. 12.

17. Ibid., p. 16.

18. Ibid., p. 31.

19. R. J. Henle, "Energy Policy: A Matter of Life and Death," *America,* 14 February 1981, p. 122.

20. Ward, *Progress,* p. 126.

21. Henle, p. 122.

22. Heilbroner, *The Worldly Philosophers,* p. 303.

23. Avery Dulles, "The Meaning of Faith Considered in Relationship to Justice," in *The Faith That Does Justice,* ed. J. C. Haughey (New York: Paulist Press, 1977), pp. 10-46.

24. John Rawls, *A Theory of Justice* (Cambridge, Mass.: Harvard University Press, 1971), p. 303.

25. Peter Singer, "Famine, Affluence, and Morality," in *Social Ethics,* ed.

T. A. Mappes and J. S. Zembaty (New York: McGraw-Hill, Inc., 1977), p. 317.

26. Ibid., p. 319.

27. Ward, *The Home of Man*, p. 5.

28. Dulles, p. 32.

29. Ibid., p. 13.

30. Ibid., p. 37.

31. Ibid., p. 44.

32. Lawrence Kohlberg, "Moral Stages and Moralization," in *Moral Development and Behavior*, ed. Thomas Lickona (New York: Holt, Rinehart & Winston, 1976), p. 49.

Bibliography

Botstein, L. "The Vienna Analogy." *The New Republic*, 20 December 1980, pp. 26-28.

Boyer, E. L. "The College Curriculum: Our Search for Common Ground." *Chicago Tribune*, 23 November 1978, p. 10.

Dulles, Avery. "The Meaning of Faith Considered in Relationship to Justice." In *The Faith That Does Justice*, edited by J. C. Haughey, pp. 10-46. New York: Paulist Press, 1977.

Greene, W. "Triage." *New York Times Magazine*, 5 January 1975, pp. 9-11, 44-45, 51.

Hardin, G. "Living on a Lifeboat." In *Social Ethics*, edited by T. A. Mappes and J. S. Zembaty, pp. 322-331. New York: McGraw-Hill Book Co., 1977.

Harrington, Michael. *Decade of Decision.* New York: Simon & Schuster, 1980.

Heilbroner, Robert. *The Future as History.* New York: Harper, 1959.

————. *An Enquiry into the Human Prospect.* New York: W. W. Norton & Co., 1974.

————. *The Worldly Philosophers.* 5th ed. New York: Simon & Schuster, 1980.

Henle, R. J. "Energy Policy: A Matter of Life and Death." *America*, 14 February 1981, pp. 121-123.

Kohlberg, Lawrence. "Moral Stages and Moralization." In *Moral Development and Behavior*, edited by Thomas Lickona, pp. 31-53. New York: Holt, Rinehart & Winston, 1976.

Lasch, Christopher. *The Culture of Narcissism.* New York: W. W. Norton & Co., Warner Books, 1979.

McCarthy. C. "A Future Already Forgotten." *Chicago Tribune*, 24 February 1981, section 2, p. 3.

Rawls, John. *A Theory of Justice.* Cambridge, Mass.: Harvard University Press, 1971.

Singer, Peter. "Famine, Affluence, and Morality." In *Social Ethics,* edited by T. A. Mappes and J. S. Zembaty, pp. 315-322. New York: McGraw-Hill Book Co., 1977.

Ward, Barbara. *The Home of Man.* New York: W. W. Norton & Co., 1976.

————. *Progress for a Small Planet.* New York: W. W. Norton & Co., 1979.

Ward, Barbara and Dubos, Rene. *Only One Earth.* New York: W. W. Norton & Co., 1972.

MINISESSION C

Father Thomas McMahon, C.S.V.: The overall theme of the Loyola-Baumgarth Symposium is Faith and Justice. Faith and justice are more than theoretical concepts. They are the reality of things that must be passed on from one generation to another. Faith and justice entail a moral sense that necessarily changes as circumstances change. We live in a changing community. The Chicago black community, the census tells us, is changing dramatically. High-rises for the elderly are being built throughout the city. The baby boom, which once influenced our educational institutions so significantly, is now subsiding. Hispanics are a major new force. These are just a few of the changes that are taking place. What is the faith which is to be passed on to these people? How is it to be passed on? What new sense of justice is appropriate for these changing circumstances?

Dr. Gerald Gutek is the speaker at this session. Being a historian, he is intent upon uncovering a usable past, which identifies the faith and justice that will be reliable guides for the present and the future. How can the perennial values of rationality and Jesuit humanism, he asks, be applied today? Dr. Gutek received all his degrees in higher education at the University of Illinois, Champaign. He is the author of seven books and numerous articles and book reviews. He has spoken many times at meetings of professional organizations. He came to Loyola University in 1963 as a historian of education in the department of the foundations of education. He has been the dean of the School of Education since 1979. He was named "Educator of the Year" by the Loyola Chapter of Phi Delta Kappa in 1977.

I present to you Dr. Gerald Gutek.

Revitalizing the Loyola University Heritage: The Challenge
Dr. Gerald L. Gutek

The arguments in my paper rest on the simple but basic assumption that an institution, like a person, has a past, which to some extent shapes its character and influences its future. As an individual, living at a particular time and place, each of us has his own continuing biography. The institutions that we serve also have their own biographies, which are more accurately called institutional histories. Just as an individual's biography is the result of social interaction, so an institutional history records a particular institution's impact on the social order of which it is a part. Obvious but important distinctions between an individual's biography and an institutional history are: (1) the biography of a person, although involving relationships with other persons, focuses on the life of a single individual; (2) although individuals have a significant role in shaping an institution, most institutions have a corporate experience and a much longer transgenerational life span.

It can be asserted further that the character of an institution arises from its historically evolved corporate existence. To an extent an institution at any given moment is what it has been. Healthy and growing institutions need a conscious and dynamic heritage that can be continually enriched. To use the meeting of challenges as opportunities for institutional development, an institution must have a usable past that serves as an instrument to chart future directions.[1] For the members of the Loyola University community, a usable institutional heritage is a past about which we are conscious and reflective as students, faculty, staff, and administrators. A usable past can be revitalized and reconstructed in the face of present and future challenges. In pursuing the theme of a usable institutional heritage, the remainder of the paper will focus on three interrelated objectives. One, it will examine the Loyola University heritage by identifying and defining the perennial values that contribute to its character and to its mission of faith and justice.[2] Two, it will relate these perennial values to Loyola's institutional place and function in an urban American social order. Three, it will suggest the continuation and reconstruction of these values in terms of the challenges that we face as an independent, urban, Catholic, and Jesuit university.

Perennial values are recurrent over the course of human history. Like a tree that sprouts, blossoms, and bears fruit each year, perennial values are manifested and recur in each human generation. Growing in a particular place, trees are nourished by the soil of a particular environment. Loyola University's perennial values blossomed and were nourished by the soil of Western civilization. It is from that civilization that several strands of perennial values have developed that contribute to Loyola University's institutional heritage and character. A cultural contribution to our heritage from classical Greece and Rome, the first strand affirms that rationality is a defining characteristic of human nature and that human beings are true to their nature when governed by their rationality. Although Platonic and Aristotelian metaphysical and epistemological nuances differ, they assert the primacy and power of human rationality. The rational nature of human beings was reasserted later in Western history by Augustine and Aquinas. Within the conditions of human and physical nature, persons can define a large part of their individual, social, and institutional lives by exercising their rationality in framing alternatives, weighing and reflecting on these alternatives, and choosing to act upon them. This means that, while recognizing the power of nonrational, social, biological, and psychological determinants over persons, we expressly recognize that human rationality gives us our freedom and the responsibility of self-determination as persons and societies. This does not mean that our recognition and affirmation of reason should be cold, austere, unfeeling, or even dryly academic, but that we see human freedom as flowing from our rationality. A university should be an institution where faculty and students use reason to examine human experience and to multiply by their research, teaching, and learning alternatives that promote personal and social growth.

A second strand of perennial values makes Loyola University

a Christian and Catholic institution. In no uncertain terms these values embody the commitment of a faith community to the idea that human beings are endowed with a spiritual nature by a personal, caring Creator whom they are destined to see and experience. It means that Jesus Christ—both in his historical presence and as Redeemer—is the Ideal Exemplar. The Christian presence manifests humankind's twofold spiritual and rational characteristics, not as an irreconcilable dualism, but as complementary dimensions of human nature. Because we are spiritual, we enjoy a personal dignity and are destined for salvation. Because we are physical, we have our own biographies that make us discrete but unite us to generations past, present, and to come. A Catholic Christian university then should manifest a faith commitment that demonstrates the underlying values that give it a unique character. The faith commitment means that spirituality and religious experience are prized as being worthy of sustained research, study, and teaching. It also means that the institutional environment or milieu will facilitate the celebration of the religious dimension of human experience.

A third strand of perennial values arises from the fact that Loyola University is a Jesuit institution of higher learning. Established and continued by the Society of Jesus, Loyola University shares the tradition of Christian humanism that is associated with Ignatius Loyola and the intellectual, religious, and social currents of the late Renaissance and Reformation periods. The Ignatius heritage of Christian humanism means that: (1) the spirituality of educated persons is not confined to the quiet of the cloister but is manifested in the world; (2) both spirituality and rationality are integrated consciously into a concept of integrity and wholeness; (3) the Christian humanist is a person of many concerns whose view is catholic in the broad sense of cosmopolitan and universal.

To summarize then: the perennial values I have identified recognize, prize, and encourage the university's commitment to human rationality and spirituality. Not isolated and disconnected entities, these perennial values are orchestrated in the Ignatian vision of the Christian humanist.

The foregoing statement of perennial values is general; it ought to be valid for Jesuit universities throughout the world. Loyola University of Chicago, however, has its own biography based on its own time and place. As well as being a Catholic and

Jesuit institution of higher learning in the general sense, Loyola University is an independent, urban, American university, located in Chicago, Illinois, and having a history dating from 1871. Late nineteenth- and twentieth-century Chicago was not and is not Medieval or Renaissance Europe. Chicago's metropolitan area was and is a rapidly changing, urban, and continually emerging society. The theme of revitalizing the Loyola heritage calls upon the members of the university community to recognize and maintain the institution's perennial value core, but also to readapt, broaden, and reconstruct these essential values in creating a still larger value synthesis.

In its 110-year history, the reconstruction of the institution's perennial values has taken three major directions. First, institutionally, Loyola University has responded to the challenges of American social and economic development by preparing educated persons who could appropriate and use knowledge to direct the course of an industrializing, urbanizing, and modernizing society. In this way knowledge was and is put into the service of human beings.

Second, Loyola University accepted the challenge of providing higher education, true to standards of academic excellence, to the upwardly mobile children of immigrants when this responsibility was virtually ignored by public, state, and land-grant colleges and universities. The continuation and the reconstruction of this commitment pose a major contemporary challenge to the university. While the students attending Loyola University still represent a variety of ethnic and racial backgrounds, the later generations of European Catholic ethnic groups no longer appear to identify their educational needs as exclusively or as directly with the urban Catholic university as they did in the past. Providing a quality academic education to currently disadvantaged but upwardly mobile ethnic and racial groups such as Hispanics and black Americans remains a paramount challenge. It is one, however, with which Loyola University has had a successful experience historically. It is a challenge that needs to be met with the same sense of social justice and also with the same dedication to quality that exemplified Loyola's service to the children of the new Americans of past generations.

The third challenge that has an impact on the perennial values and the sense of justice relates to the function of the university in modern society—an issue faced by all universities. This continuing issue, which became acute during the "activist" period of the late 1960s and early 1970s, centered on the degree to which Loyola and other universities were to become agencies of programmatic and active social and political change.

The issue also might be viewed as an attempt to determine the relationship between the pursuit of knowledge as a function of scholarly research, teaching, and learning, and the programmatic role that a university might exercise as an agency of social change. When student activism subsided in the early 1970s, the urgency of the issue also subsided. It remains a now hidden but still real and unresolved tension of university life. And it is an issue that touches on knowledge and values, faith and justice, in the university.

In working toward a conclusion, I want to identify several major challenges that face us as members of the Loyola University community. Further, I would see these challenges as raising the possibility of revitalizing certain identifying institutional characteristics or "givens," namely, that as participants in the Western cultural tradition, we recognize and celebrate our spirituality and rationality. As participants in the Jesuit educational tradition, we endorse the embodiment of these values within the integrating context of Christian humanism.

True to its commitment to faith and justice, Loyola University faces the challenge of aiding in the renewal of urban life and of assisting currently educationally-disadvantaged groups to participate fully in the American Dream. In its undergraduate and professional schools, the university assisted the upward mobility of the children of European immigrants in the past. The credentials of many physicians, lawyers, dentists, teachers, administrators, and business, political, and educational leaders in the Chicago area include the earning of one or more degrees at Loyola University.

Is it possible for Loyola University to aid once more in extending the American Dream to other urban groups as it did for the children of European immigrants? An answer predicated on social justice would be an emphatic *yes!* But as experience teaches, good will, enthusiasm, and a sense of justice, while necessary, are insufficient for meeting a challenge on a sustained basis. Knowledge, accurate data, planning, and resources are needed as well. We need to probe and reconstruct the historically evolved but largely unconscious memory of Loyola University as an urban institution. Specifically we need to generate questions and answers in terms of Loyola University's mission. While the *we* involves the entire university community, the expertise of the faculties in history and the social sciences would be particularly invaluable in dealing with such questions as:

1. Historically, who really attended Loyola University? What socioeconomic, ethnic, and religious groups used our university in the past?

2. Is it possible to generalize a model or models of Loyola University's relationship to the socioeconomic and educational mobility of those who attended it in the past?

3. Has the student population changed in its social, economic, educational, ethnic, geographical, racial, and religious composition? If so, what is the nature of the change?

4. Who are the new ethnic, racial, social, economic, and religious groups in Chicago and the metropolitan area? How are they like, and how do they differ from, the Loyola students of the past?

5. In light of this information, how can the university community readapt and reconstruct itself to devise and implement new models that meet contemporary needs and social change?

While it is important to pose and respond to these questions, it is crucial that our queries reflect a point of view that embodies Loyola's perennial values. Our commitment to a faith and to a sense of justice makes us unique among others who might raise similar questions. It is our continuing task to reaffirm the perennial values that proclaim the human person as a spiritual and rational being. It is our task to preserve and regenerate our commitment to the ideal of Christian humanism by enlarging the concept to embrace both new challenges and solutions. It is important that we come to know ourselves by coming to know our institutional heritage. Hopefully, in doing so we will gain a usable past.

Notes

1. The author's view of a "usable past" blends the "new history" of Becker and Beard with a concept of institutional character reminiscent of Collingwood.

2. The concept of perennial values in educational philosophy is treated in Neil C. McCluskey, *Catholic Viewpoint on Education* (New York: Image Books, 1962); Gerald L. Gutek, *Philosophical Alternatives in Education* (Columbus: Charles F. Merrill Publishing Co., 1974), pp. 69-85; and by implication in the works of Robert Hutchins and Jacques Maritain.